A Handbook of Etiquettes

Published by
Lotus Press Publishers & Distributors

A Handbook of Etiquettes

Deepa Sawhney

Lotus PRESS

4735/22, Prakash Deep Building,
Ansari Road, Daryaganj,
New Delhi - 110002

Lotus Press Publishers & Distributors
Unit No.220, 2nd Floor, 4735/22, Prakash Deep Building,
Ansari Road, Daryaganj, New Delhi- 110002
Ph:- 32903912, 23280047, 098118-38000
Email : lotuspress1984@gmail.com
Visit us : www.lotuspress.co.in

A Handbook of Etiquettes

ISBN : 978-81-8382-221-3

Printed & Published by : **Lotus Press Publishers & Distributors,** New Delhi- 2

Preface

Etiquettes form an important part of how you are recieved by the society at large. Various cultures have different ideas about proper conduct and behavioural patterns. Indian society is particularly critical about the attitudes of individuals in social gatherings. The social standing of the person depends upon the etiquettes displayed by them in varying situations.

In today's world it is more important to have a universally acceptable behavioural pattern. This book is helpful to those who are unsure of themselves. It is a comprehensive guide to how one must conduct themselves in various situations - social gatherings to business meetings, interviews to attending a telephone call. Each of these have a set manner in which a person may present herself or himself. These can be grasped from the book and be utilised in developing one's personality and improving the confidence level.

In a concise and comprehensive manner the book explains to the readers how they may perform better. It is a textbook on behavioural patterns and manners that would impress the people around oneself. In other words one may call it a mannual to right attitude and proper manner in any situation without compromising one's own position.

– Author

Contents

1
Introduction

Etiquette

"Etiquette" is about presenting yourself with the kind of polish that shows you can be taken seriously. The word "etiquette" is derived from French which actual means a "ticket", your ticket to getting anything and anyplace you want.

Etiquette is a code of behaviour that influences expectations for social behaviour according to contemporary conventional norms within a society, social class, or group. Rules of etiquette are usually unwritten, but aspects of etiquette have been codified from time to time. Rule of etiquette encompass most aspects of social interaction used. A rule of etiquette may reflect an underlying ethical code, or it may reflect a person's fashion or status.

Like "culture", it is a word that has gradually grown plural, especially in a multi-ethnic society with many clashing expectation. Thus, it is now possible to refer to "an etiquette" or "a culture", realising that these may not be universal. In Britain, through, the word etiquette has its roots in the eighteenth century, becoming a universal force in the nineteenth century to the extent that it has been described as the one word that aptly describes life during the reign of Queen Victoria.

Cultural Differences

Etiquette is dependent on culture, what is excellent etiquette in one society may shock another. Etiquette evolves within culture. Etiquette can vary widely between different cultures and nations. In China, a person who takes the last item of food from a common plate or bowl without first offering it to others at the table may be seen as a glutton and insulting the generosity of the host. In America a guest is expected to eat all of the food given to him as a compliment to the quality of the cooking.

Etiquette is a topic that has occupied writers and thinkers in all sophisticated societies for millennia, beginning with a behaviour code by pathogen, a vizier in ancient Egypt's Old Kingdom during the reign of the Fifth Dynasty King Djedkare Isese (ca. 2414-2375 BC). All known literate conversations, including ancient Greece and Rome, developed rules for proper social conduct. Confucius included rules for eating and speaking along with his more philosophical sayings.

Early modern conceptions of what behaviour identifies a "gentleman" were codified in the sixteenth century, in a book by Baldassare Castiglione, II Cortegiano ("The Courtier"); its codification of expectations at the Este court remained in force in its essentials until World War I. Louis XIV established an elaborate and rigid court ceremony, but distinguished himself from the high bourgeoisie by continuing to eat, stylishly and fastidiously, with his fingers. An important book about etiquette is *Galateo, over de' costume* by Monsignor Giovanni della Casa; in fact, in Italian, is generally called galateo (or etichetta or protocollo).

In the UK, Debrett's is considered by many to be the arbiter of etiquette; their guides to manners and from have long been the last word among polite society. Traditional publications such as Correct Form have been updated to reflect contemporary society, and new titles Etiquette for Girls and Manners for Men act as guides for those who want to combine a modern lifestyle with traditional values.

In the American colonies Benjamin Franklin and George Washington wrote codes of conduct for young gentlemen. The immense popularity of advice columns and books by Letitia Baldrige and Miss Manners shows the currency of this topic. Even more recently, the rise of the Internet has necessitated the adaptation of existing rules of conduct to etiquette, which governs the drafting of email, rules for participating in an online forum, and so on.

In Germany, there is an "unofficial" code of conduct written by Adolph Freiherr Dnigge in the late 18th century entitled exactly *Uber den Umgang mit Menschen* (On Human Relations). The code of conduct is still highly respected in Germany today and is used primarily in the higher society.

Etiquette may be wielded as a social weapon. The outward adoption of the superficial mannerisms of an in-group, in the interests of social advancement rather than a concern for others, is considered by many a form of snobbery, lacking in virtue.

Why do you need to know about etiquette?

The rules of proper etiquette have been around for years but they are far more important in this day and age than ever before. Implementing proper etiquette skills into everyday life should be habit for everyone – including children. After all, a person who displays proper etiquette not only feels good about himself, he also makes those around him feel important and respected.

Did you know that an impression is made within the first seven seconds of meeting someone? Seven seconds is an extremely small amount of you must rely on your etiquette skills and social and social graces to ace that first impression. Are you up-to-date with these skills? Well, it is never to early, or too late, to start.

Having social grace means that you can maneuver through any situation with ease; whether you are in an interview or on a dinner date you will have confidence and put your companion at ease. For instance, at a dinner table, you will know which fork to use, how to eat bread, and where to place your napkin. A great example of how it feels not to know proper etiquette is in the movie Pretty Women. Remember when Julia Roberts wasn't sure how to use her appetizer utensil? She was visibly unsure of herself, and she had to look around at the other diners to figure out what to do. You can save yourself this embarrassment by becoming well versed in social etiquette.

Obviously, proper etiquette is important in a social setting, but is rucial in a business setting. In order to achieve business success, you must be able to adapt to ever changing situations and act with confidence. Displaying proper etiquette will get you noticed and, obviously, being noticed is great for business. For example: There are two people being interviewed for a top position at a large company. One is late and not dressed appropriately. What is more, he makes the mistake of not making eye contact when speaking to the interviewer. But the other prospect is early for the appointment and dressed in a suit. He also makes the effort to be assertive and eager during the interview. Who do you think will be chosen for the top position? The person who displays proper business etiquette will always have the edge in such situations!

As you can see, etiquette is an important part of everyday life. A person who displays proper etiquette shows respect for himself as well as respect for those around him. Don't you think it's about time test your social savvy?

Etiquette Rules and Regulations

1. **How to Dine?**

   When invited to a pre-arranged meal, always use your utensils from the "outside in." After all, untensils are set in the order that food will be served.

2. **Telephone Manners –**

   When calling a friend, identify yourself to the person who answer the phone before asking to speak your friend. By doing so, the parents or other family member who answer the phone will appreciate this courtesy and see you as friendly.

3. **On Correspondence –**

   Anytime it takes someone more than 15 minutes to do something for you, send the person a thank-you note. By doing so, the person will know you really appreciated what was done for you.

4. **Be Gracious –**

   When you are sent an invitation that requires an RSVP, be sure to let the person know if you will be able to go to the gathering. After all, "RSVP" means "respond if you please."

5. **Shoes are Important –**

   When getting dressed each day, be sure that your

shoes are well-maintained. People associate the way you take care of your shoes with the way you handle detail in the rest of your life.

6. **Be Open to New Foods –**

When you are invited out to eat and are served a food that is not your favourite, try a piece of it anyway. You may be surprised and find that you end up liking it.

7. **Ask Questions –**

When talking with friends and family, always make a point of asking them questions about themselves. People will see you as interesting if you are interested in them.

8. **At the Table –**

When eating a roll, be sure to break-off a bite-sized piece at a time. No bread-and-butter sandwiches please.

9. **Be Friendly –**

When you are in school, be cool by making a point to talk with that new kid in your class. If the tables were turned, wouldn't that make you feel good?

10. **The Rule of Twelve –**

When talking with others, always use a form of thanks and the person's name in the first 12 words you speak ("It's good to see you Minni", or "Thanks for picking me up from soccer, Dad.") By following this rule of 12, people will want to continue to do nice things for you.

11. **Dining Out –**

- When decanting wine, make sure that you tilt the paper cup, and pour slowly so as not to "bruise the fruit of the wine."

- If drinkir g directly from the bottle, always hold it with your fingers covering the label.

12 Entertaining in Your Home –

- A centerpiece for the table should never be anything prepared by a taxidermist.
- Do not allow the dog to eat at the table....no matter how good his manners are?

13. Personal Hygiene –

- While ears need to be cleaned regularly, this is a job that should be done in private using one's OWN truck keys.
- Proper use of toiletries can forestall bathing for several days. However, if you live alone, deodorant is a waste of good money.
- Dirt and grease under the fingernails is a social no-no, as they tend to detract from a women's jewelry and alter the taste of finger foods.

14. Dating (outside the family) –

- Always offer to bait your date's hook, especially on the first date.
- Be aggressive. Let her know you're interested: "I've been wanting to go out with you since I read that stuff on the bathroom wall two years ago."
- Establish with her parents what time she is expected back.
- Some will say 10:00 PM: others might say "Monday". If the latter is the answer, it is the man's responsibility to get her school on time.

❑❑❑

2
Social Etiquettes

Social etiquettes are mannerisms (which can either be in visual, written, vocal or combined) that are socially acceptable to the society, which leaves a good, clear and long lasting impression on the recipient. It is the main tool of self-development. It given you a special place in the public gathering because of your good and gentle behaviour; you get to know well and will come across good and polished people with your behaviour.

In order to avoid making any unintentional faux pas, read the below mentioned social etiquettes that are in tune with the general Indian manners and protocol:

Faux Pas

A faux pas is a violation of accepted social rules (for example, standard customs or etiquette rules). Faux pas vary widely from culture to culture, and what is considered good manners in one culture can be considered a faux pas in another. The term comes originally from French, and literally mean "false step".

1. It is contemptible to bring together recently separated or divorced persons with your other single friends, solely for the purpose of "fixing them up" with someone.
2. If things go wrong with the hired help, never criticize them in public.
3. A handshake is not a universally approved greeting.
4. "Look'em right in the eye" is not always applicable.
5. What Americans call 'diapers' are called napkins, in England. This could lead to some hilarious or embarrassing misunderstandings.
6. Avoid sending alcohol to a person's office. Most companies prohibit alcohol consumption on the job.
7. Never send a gift to the office of an editor reporter, etc., to thank them for favourable publicity, as it looks more like a payoff.
8. Never carry away cutlery, towels, ash-trays, etc., from hotels where they are kept for the use of guests.
9. Now-a-days, gallantry in the corporate culture will get you nowhere (as far as gender rules are concerned), except perhaps into hot water.
10. Never wear skirts and trousers that are so tight as to convey a message of sexiness.
11. Exposed cleavage and miniskirts are not appropriate business attire for a woman.
12. Do not give false compliments, and do not lie to people at social functions to be polite. People can detect your insincerity, no matter how well you act.

13. Do not ask food or drink at a meeting unless they are being offered.
14. Printed thank-you cards or notes from a gift shop are not gestures acceptable as token of gratitude. Gratitude does not come pre-packaged.

Etiquette Tidbits

1. The use of "please", "Thank you", "You're welcome", "Excuse me" let people know that you have good manners.
2. Look people in the eye when you speak to them.
3. When you are introduced, stand up and say, "Nice to meet you" or "Hello," or "How do you do?"
4. If your child asks you, "What is the worst, thing a person can do?" your answer should be, "To hurt someone's feelings."
5. The most important things about introductions is to actually make them.
6. Join in a conversation to make a meal more enjoyable.
7. Start eating only when everyone is seated and has been served.
8. If you drop something during a meal at home, pick it up. At a friend's house, leave it until the meal is over, then pick it up.
9. If you have to blow your nose, or dislodge something stuck between your teeth, excuse yourself and leave the table.
10. If someone drops his/her books or papers in the corridor, it is good manners to stop and help,

especially when everyone is hustling to get to the next class.

Managing Relationships

1. Always be gracious in all your dealings with people.
2. Handle all unpleasant and sticky situations with tact and gentleness.
3. Always be helpful and amicable with your friends, for true friendship is everlasting.
4. In matters of monetary help to friends, be extra careful.
5. Never take your friends for granted. Do not be possessive about them or patronize them.
6. Learn to respect the feelings and moods of others.
7. When a person or family moves into a vacant house nearby, you could call on them to establish cordial relations.
8. If someone indulges in gossip, it is best to keep a safe distance from that person.
9. If you value your privacy, and find your neighbour bothering you with frequent visits, you can politely tell him/her that you will spend a longer time with him/her later when you have time.
10. Treat your assistants and juniors with candour and friendliness without going overboard. Be careful that you do not become too bossy or snobbish.
11. With servants, you have to be strict without being rude or cruel, being sensitive to their needs and background.

12. It is charitable to give servants that they need every now and then without grumbling. Ensure that their need is genuine.
13. A teacher should be strict while dealing with students, without being harsh. A teacher should also be patient with them and should not discriminate between students.
14. The students should show respect and deference to their teachers. They should conduct themselves well and ensure that they merit the attention of their teacher.
15. If you are a customer in a shop, treat the shopkeeper with deference, for he is not your servant.
16. Do not unnecessarily waste the shopkeeper's time, by asking him to show you everything and then walk out empty-handed.
17. Do not bargain if you see a signboard suggesting that prices are fixed.
18. As a shopkeeper, always greet your customers with a smile.
19. Attend to your customers promptly, and if there is a big crowd, acknowledge the presence of the person trying to catch your attention with a nod, telling him/her, "Just a minute, I'll attend to you in a minute."
20. The parent-child relationship is very important, and children normally emulate their parents.
21. As a parent, be patient with your child, listen to him/her patiently, and make him/her feel loved. Inculcate human values right from childhood.

22. Establish a healthy relationship with children, so that they are able to communicate with you easily.
23. Ensure that your child shows deference to elders, and is always polite with them.
24. If a child throws tantrums, treat with iron gloves, making sure that the child knows that he/she cannot have his/her way.
25. Always encourage your children in all their endeavours.
26. Do not show favouritism amongst your children as this will only lead to an inferiority complex in the others.

Giving and Receiving Gifts

1. It is very important that you give and receive gifts graciously.
2. If you receive a gift with an expression of gratitude, the giver will appreciate it very much for he/she has spend time and thought on the selection of the gift.
3. Joke gifts may evoke laughter at that moment, but can leave a sour taste.
4. By nicely wrapping a gift and giving it on time you enhance the value of the gift and your gesture.
5. Watch out what you gift professionally for what you give sets a precedence which must be matched or exceeded in the future.
6. Receiving a nicely wrapped gift with a personal note inside is one of life's nicest experiences.
7. An employee is under no obligation to give a superior

a gift—he/she may do so at his/her discretion, or as a spontaneous act.

8. Even if a person has been thanked verbally, it is always good to follow it up with a 'Thank-you note."
9. Gifts for babies can include pins, mugs, rattles, clothes, silver or gold objects, dresses, albums, baby blanket, music box, or simple toys.
10. Children would love to receive books, toys, craft kits, educational games, sports items, paints and brushes, and video games.
11. Teenagers love books, clothes, audio and video cassettes, sport equipment, camera, watch, etc.
12. For weddings one can present silverware, art objects, money, glassware or pottery, table lamps or brassware, wall hangings, linen, engraved boxes or jewellery boxes, thermoware, like flasks or casseroles, etc.
13. Generally, for anniversaries, gifts are given only on special anniversaries such as a 25th year anniversary.
14. The most suitable gift for anniversaries would be flowers and bouquets, or a basketful of assorted fruits.

Slipping Away

1. It is important that you close the conversation gracefully.
2. It is equally aggravating when people just drift away while the conversation is going on, without some acknowledgement that a conversation has occurred.
3. If you do have to move away, wait for a break in the

conversation, then say, "Well, I have to say hello to our chief guest. Can we carry on this discussion some other time?"

4. If, for some reason, it is not possible to end the conversation properly, make some sort of parting gesture, like an eye contact and a wave.

Keeping the Conversation Going

1. Learn to lend your ears, and listen to the person speaking patiently, without butting in every now and then.
2. Keep eye contact so that the person knows that your attention is focused on what he is saying.
3. Try to ask open-ended questions that will keep the conversation going.

   e.g. "Why did you come to this decision?" or "How did you manage to escape?" which might only have an answer in "Yes" or "No".
4. People like to be asked their opinion concerning major events.

   e.g. "The twin towers of World Trade Centre were bombed. Do you think Osama Bin Laden had a hand in this?"
5. Try to change the topic, if it gets boring, in a discreet manner, e.g. "Talking of bombing.......what is your opinion about the Taliban?"
6. Do not rush through your conversation. This shows you are anxious that you might not get a chance to give your opinion.

7. Do not talk very slowly and with too many pauses, leaving the other person to finish sentences for you.
8. You have every right to disagree about something only do not let it drift into a squabble!

Making Small Talk

1. First size up the person with whom you are going to converse.
2. Smile, make eye contact and shake hands.
3. Introduce yourself, and listen carefully to the other persons name.
4. Repeat the other person's so that you will not easily forget it.
5. You may start the conversation by saying something about youself, your work, your family, etc.
6. You need not hesitate to confess that you are a shy person—"Big parties like this intimidate me," or "I making the first overtures."

Delivering Small Speech

1. When you step on to the dais to deliver a speech, and feel very nervous about it just remember that the audience is on your side, and that they want you to be as relaxed as they are.
2. Breathe, inhaling through the nose exhaling through the mouth.
3. Since the stage freight involves the right-side of the brain to function, counter it with some function of the left-side, such as counting or working some problems in your head.

4. Do not forget to smile—you will feel the tension melting away.
5. Get ready for your talk, ensuring that everything has been prepared in advance—now you want your audience to perceive you, your gestures and voice modulations, whether you want to welcome, motivate, instruct the audience, or explain some situation, or extol a person, a company, etc.
6. Speak while standing, whenever possible.
7. Adjust your talk according to the interests of the audience and sprinkle your talk with humorous anecdotes.
8. Try to be at par with the audience level, without sounding snobbish or self-bragging or hostile.
9. Remember that the audience would like to hear you present the speech or information, rather than just read it from a paper.
10. Be specific about the points you make.
11. Speak clearly and with feeling and enthusiasm.
12. Control your voice—a first-timer will tend to speak loudly or shout due to nervousness.
13. Speak slowly, so that people can follow what you are stating.
14. Avoid rambling and repeating.
15. Keep your talk brief and to the point.
16. When you have finished, say, "Thank you," and sit down.

17. Since first impressions are so vital, open your address by complimenting the audience, or making some provocative or shocking statement, or narrating a joke, etc.
18. Since the last impressions too are of significance, do not be afraid to employ some dramatic or emotional language, or use some lines of stirring poetry or ghazal.
19. If you are introducing a speaker on the podium to the audience, make it brief, and leave yourself out of it as much as possible.

Delivering Bad News

1. If some calamity befalls someone you know, acknowledge the misfortune at the earliest opportunity.
2. If you are attending a funeral, offer your condolences, by simply saying, "I'm very sorry about your loss, or simply, "I'm sorry."
3. When someone is giving you bad news and giving you details about it, remain silent and listen to him attentively, and at the appropriate time you can say e.g something soothing like, "It must be a taxing period for you, I am sorry."
4. Do not relate another similar incident, where the other person is suffering even more, for that gives the impression of one-upmanship, making him/her feel worse.
5. Remember that it is no time for unsolicited advice.

6. Do not pry into the other person's trouble. Let him volunteer to tell you whatever he wants you to know.
7. You can share in your colleagues grief at the work arena which may be fraught with difficult situations, by assuring your colleague that he/she is not alone, and you stand by him.
8. Never say, "I told you such a thing would happen, "or "Everything will work out for the best." Instead you could say, "I'm sorry you have to go through this," or "is there anything I can do to help?"
9. If you are sexually harassed, it is best to deal with the abuser by pricking his/her ego, by saying something like, "I'm sure you don't think that was sexually attractive. In fact, it was so comical! You are truly making a fool of yourself." Or "You were pathetic, you silly man/woman," or "I am going to forget this happened, but if you repeat this, believe me, you are going to be in more trouble than you can imagine."
10. If you are in an embarrassing situation, where someone's fly is open, the sari has stepped down off the shoulder, or someone has bad breath, you can directly, but discreetly, say to the person out of earshot of other people, "Your fly is open," "Your pallau has fallen away," or "I think you need to gargle your mouth with a mouth wash."
11. If you do not know the person, directly find someone who can convey the message.
12. Never ever ask the following inappropriate questions: "How much money do you make?" "How come you do not have any children?"

13. "Are you two sleeping together?" If someone does ask you such a question, your favourite tactic should be, "why do you ask?"
14. When someone is going to repeat an often repeated story, you can say, Oh, that story about you losing your spectacles? Well, that is really hilarious!" and jump in with a new topic of conversation.
15. When someone is verbally attacking your friend who is not there, you can cut short that criticism by saying, "I am sure he/she has a different story to tell. Let us not go into it now."
16. When someone is cracking some vulgar jokes, you can discreetly move away, saying, "I don't think I want to hear this".
17. Have a sense of self-worth and a respect for others which will help you accept criticism without rancour, and deal with conflict without being cowed down by it.

Deaths and Funerals

1. When tragedy strikes a near one, the most important chore is to inform all the relatives, friends and colleagues and all those who were close to him/her.
2. Offer whatever help you can to the bereaved family.
3. Offer your condolences to all those affected by the death of their near ones.
4. You may not be able to express your grief to them, but try to speak from your heart which will have a genuine ring to it.

5. You can carry some flowers or a garland or a wreath that you can place over the body.
6. Avoid wearing bright-coloured clothes, heavy makeup and jewellery. Sober clothes, preferably, in white, black, or some pastel shade would do.
7. Try to avoid talking children to funerals as they may not know the seriousness of the occasion.
8. If you are in a distant place, send a letter of heartfelt appropriate time.

Office Parties

1. Since seniors and juniors get together at office parties. Usually juniors are hesitant in mixing with their peers. Make sure everyone is at ease, and intermingle freely.
2. The host should welcome everyone individually.
3. Punctuality is a must in such parties. Women should, be businesslike at such parties, though they may move and talk freely amongst their male colleagues.
4. Be careful that no one gets inebriated and makes a nuisance of himself.

Children's Party

1. Always remember that children, are very energetic, and so like to have a lot of entertainment and amusement.
2. The occasion can be a birthday, a naming ceremony, the birth of a baby, or just about anything.
3. Children normally like to give and receive presents, so ensure that if your child receives presents from others, he or she gives them something in return.

4. The guests should include the neighbourhood kids also. Include even those with whom your child is not very friendly, so that the other child does not feel hurt and lift out.
5. The invitees can be invited either verbally or by sending them the readily available special printed invitation cards.
6. It is always good to let the parents of the children know when the party is likely to begin and end, so that they can arrange to take them home.
7. For the children's party, punctuality should be observed. Otherwise your child might miss some of the recreational games that have been arranged for them.
8. Ensure that you have a reward for each game that is played.
9. After the cake is cut (or, whatever the occasion, when it ends), see that the children have their plates filled and that each one has a place to sit.
10. If your child is a guest, make sure that he/she thanks the friends and their parents before taking leave of them.

Party Time for Adults

1. Generally speaking, a party is a good time to relax and meet everyone.
2. You need not have any reason for having a party, though birthdays, anniversaries and engagements are good enough reasons.

3. Regarding your mix of guests, it is good to combine some familiar faces with new ones.
4. Avoid shop talk that may exclude other guests, and try including everyone in the conversation.
5. Try to have a mix of non-stop talkers with silent ones, so that you eliminate a cacophony of noises from all corners of the room.
6. Courtesy demands that you send a written invitation to the invitees, unless you are very close to the person.
7. If you have accepted the invitation for the party, and are unable to attend it at the last moment, ring up and apologies to your host.
8. Cook food that is simple, tested and tasty.
9. Let there be some varieties so that people have a choice.
10. If you are serving non-vegetarian fare, be sure to include vegetarian items for those who abstain from eating non-vegetarian dishes.
11. As the host or hostess, make sure that you welcome each guest individually, dividing your time equally between them, ensuring they are all being serve food and drinks, and they are at ease.
12. Arriving very late at a party is unforgivable, so arrive well in time to join the others.
13. If you have a guest staying with you, it would be uncivil to take him/her along to the party without letting your host knows well in advance.

14. It is always good to leaves at a reasonable hour.
15. Be profuse in your thanks to your host. Compliment him/her on their choice of food, décor, etc.

Etiquettes for Occasions

1. If your guests leave with the overall impression of having been warmly welcomed by gracious people, and of having had a fine time, then you have entertained well.
2. What matters most, apart from exuding warmth, is to have everything neat and clean.
3. You do not have to make purchases with whatever you have.
4. If you are not good in cooking, and are not confident about providing a good meal, opt for a catering restaurant, that will supply a good meal.
5. When you feel that you cannot handle the party all alone, you can rope in a friend who would be willing to help you out.
6. You can host a party where you can bring together people who do not know each other but who will probably enjoy meeting one another.
7. Sometimes, it is nice to have old friends together who never seem to get an opportunity to be together.
8. Do not invite someone who you consider will not fit into the group of invitees.
9. Try always to include a person who loves to talk, can be a good conservationist, and will amuse a handful of people and get others talking as well.

10. When an unexpected guest drops by, try to accommodate him/her in a graceful and cheerful manner.
11. You can invite your guests by telephone, saving your time, and getting a quick response.
12. Make your voice welcoming and inviting, and give details about who all are being invited, the date of the party and the reason for it.
13. When you are accepting an invitation, respond before asking who else will be present at the party.
14. If you are getting food catered for the party, you can opt for those who also supply plates, cutlery, etc. with the food, or else use your own crockery and just order for the food.
15. If you include drinks, ensure that the drinks session gets over well in time for dinner.
16. While purchasing the drinks, you do not need to be extravagant and elegant, but be generous and see that there is enough.
17. Where drinks are served chilled, ensure that they are bought well in advance to have them chilled.
18. It is the host's duty to make sure the glasses are replenished.

Visiting Others

1. When you go as a guest to someone else's house, always carry something for your host and hostess, or even their children, like fruits, toys, sweets etc.
2. If you have to share the room with your host's children, so be it. Do not make a fuss.

3. If you have reservations about certain types of food that you take, let your host know in advance.
4. Never invite your relatives or friends to meet you at your host's house; it would be better for you to visit them instead.
5. Avoid taking your pets with you.
6. You should be careful in handling your host's children. Avoid criticising or disciplining them.
7. Ensure that your own children behave well. Avoid unpleasantness.
8. Always keep the room you occupy neat and clean, with your bed made up, before you leave the room. Offer you services to your host/hostess while they are engaged in cooking, washing dishes, laying the table, dusting etc.
9. You can also offer to shop for groceries, fruit and vegetables, etc.
10. If you have to share the bathroom with your hosts family, wait till the school-going children and office going people, who are rushed for time, have finished using it.
11. Avoid using the telephone, unless absolutely necessary, and them make it short, and offer to pay for it.
12. You may tip the servants at the end of your stay. When you return home, etiquette demands that you send your host a simple thank-you card or note.

Treatment of Guests

1. It is always a welcome sight for the visitors or guests to see their host/hostess at the door.

2. It would be courteous to help the guests with their luggage and show them to their room.
3. After indicating the location of the bathroom and toilet, you must immediately offer them refreshments.
4. Try to make your guests feel at home.
5. In case you do not have a spare bedroom to accommodate them, or else place them in your own room (if they are there to stay for a while) instead of in the drawing room.
6. These matters should be settled before the guests, arrival.
7. Fresh flowers add to the character of the rooms.
8. Several refreshments during the day for the guests must be offered.
9. Before they retire for the night, you can ask them if they would like an early cup of morning tea.
10. In the process of preparing special dishes for them, do not spend all your time in the kitchen. It is bad manners to leave your guests on their own all day long.
11. When you take your guests sightseeing or shopping, courtesy demands that you pay for everything, except the shopping.
12. It would be courteous to give your guests some gifts, which can be simple, like some homemade pickles or jams, or else some utility item.

Advice for Women Travelling Alone

1. Always make sure you are on an eq l footing with men.

2. Do not be afraid to talk to strangers, for they might become the most interesting part of your trip—just be wary of putting yourself in jeopardy
3. If you are not interested in communicating with someone, just respond by a nod, a smile, or monosyllabic answers.
4. In the dining room, do not be afraid to pull up a manager about discriminatory practices if you think it is warranted, but do so quietly, yet firmly.
5. If you agree to dine with a man, be sure to dine in the hotel dining room, and charge your meal to your room, thus avoiding any miscommunication about the nature of the date.
6. In your room, check your windows and door locks, and ensure that the telephone is in working order.
7. Never admit anyone to your room when you have not invited or requested through the hotel-repairman, plumber-without calling the front desk first.

Racquet Games

1. While at the tennis court, you can help out or even instruct beginners.
2. If you are not sure of a rule, it is okay to ask others for guidance.
3. Verbal and non-verbal temper tantrums should be avoided on the court.
4. Never make a fuss excuses for a bad game such as the weather, you partner or health, when in fact you were plainly outplayed.

5. Do not find excuses for a bad game such as the weather, you partner or health, when in fact you were plainly outplayed.
6. Extravagance is bad manners in most situations and particularly in sports.

Etiquette at the Pool

1. When the pool is busy, lap swimmers should stay in their lane.
2. If you are not in a group, try to find a lane or area that is not being used by a lap swimmer.
3. The best etiquette in swimming is behaving cautiously.
4. Use the wading area, if you cannot swim.
5. If you see a towel on a chair, it indicates that the chair is reserved.
6. Carry drinking water to the beach if it is a hot day, to prevent dehydration.
7. Never leave any trash behind on the beach.
8. Do not swim out beyond the posted limit.

Gym Etiquettes

1. It is always necessary to exercise common sense and etiquette at places of exercise.
2. Each participant must be sensitive to the needs of others, and try to minimise distractions and promote safety.
3. Dress sensibly while exercising
4. Ensure that you do not leave your belongings scattered around.

5. If you see someone waiting to use a particular exerciser, do not jump ahead of the person before you are in a tearing hurry it is better to skip it than jump your turn.
6. If you are using equipment, do not dally and dip another person waiting for it.
7. Avoid grunting, groaning or moaning as they are distracting and only theatrical.
8. Respect the trainers expertise and time.

Sportsmanship

1. A good sportsperson plays by the rules.
2. He/she always gives opponents the benefit of doubt.
3. A true sportsperson is concerned about everybody's safety.
4. He/she is gracious in both triumph and defeat.

Addressing People and Envelopes

1. For women 'Ms.' is the correct form of address in the business arena, and widely accepted in the social world.
2. When writing to a known person, using your first name only.
3. Never use a title for yourself while signing.
4. If your name is unisex, help the reader by including (Ms., Miss, Mrs. or Mr. to the left of your signature in parentheses.
5. All social envelopes should be addressed, written by hand, or typed.

6. Middle names are not always written out on formal envelopes.
7. When addressing an envelope to a married couple, the woman's name goes first.
8. When both halves of a couple are doctors, the envelope must be addressed as The Doctors Cherian, or Dr. Eliza Cherian and Dr. Thomas Cherian.
9. If only the husband is a doctor, then the address should read as Dr. and Mrs. Thomas Cherian, or Dr. Thomas Cherina and Mrs. Eliza Cherian (the name with the title here goes first).
10. When addressing an envelope to a boy, write 'Master' until the age of eight, and 'Mr' at eighteen.
11. Judges are referred to as "The Honourable."
12. Ambassadors are referred to as 'His/her Excellency.

Receiving Criticism

1. If there is any justification in a criticism, accept it gracefully, and make it clear that you will settle the problem.
2. If the criticism is unjustified, do not fly handle that will make you regret later. Put off the discussion by saying, "Let us get together some time and sort this out."
3. If someone is very critical of you in the presence of others, you can stop whatever you are doing or saying, and look him in the eye for a moment, thus 'freezing' him or say something like, 'please tell me your views in private."

4. When you are unsure of the validity of the criticism, you can stall by saying, "I will need to think about it, and I will get back to you".
5. If you have erred or goofed, it is best to a apologise and say, "I never intended to......, and I am sorry to have offended you."
6. It is never good to insult people, but if you have to do it, do so with grace and style.
7. A compliment benefits both the giver and the receiver.
8. While complimenting, be sincere, otherwise it instantly destroys your credibility.
9. Be specific. e.g. "The pudding was excellent," instead of "You cook well."
10. Do not make the mistake of giving unqualified praise.
11. Do not disagree when a person is complimenting you. Just smile and say "thank you."
12. When someone compliments you on a good job, do not say, "It was nothing," for this is insulting to the other person, denoting that his/her standards are wanting.
13. Do not unilaterally add more merit to a compliment. If someone says, "The meal was good, "do not add, "Good? It was excellent ....everyone lapped it up!"
14. When a compliment has to be shared do not fail to mention that the others also deserve the credit, and acknowledge the credit.

Giving Criticism

1. Whenever you are criticizing a person for some error or blunder, you can soften the attack by being circumspect and tactful.
2. It is always good to involve the other person by using 'we' instead of I.
3. If someone criticizes you, you will tend to become defensive, but your response should be given with equanimity.
4. Avoid using the word 'but' which immediately sends up a flare and triggers a defensive reaction.
5. When criticising, talk about behaviour, and not personality.
6. Let your comments be in private, and not before a crowd which the person concerned might find humiliating.
7. Be very specific in your comments.
8. Soften the impact of your criticism by beginning with a compliment.
9. Sometime it is wiser to criticize in the from of an advice.

Talking Distance

1. Asians usually maintain some distance from their guests while conversing, unlike the Americans.
2. People in the Mediterranean and Latin countries stand so close that most people feel that their space is being violated, and involuntarily step back.

3. Do not touch the arm or hand of an Asian while you are talking with one. An Asian usually resents being touched.

Hotel Services

1. If you are booking into a luxury hotel, ensure that it is done well in advance.
2. If the doorman hails a cab for you, given him a tip.
3. Tipping a porter or bell-boy is also allowed.
4. When you are shown to your room, make sure that you have the requisite towels, pillows, blankets, hangers, water to drink, etc.
5. If you are travelling on business, place your breakfast order the night before, allowing yourself plenty of time.
6. Be careful that you do not keep cash or valuables in your hotel room.
7. Check out after indicating to the reception your plans well before check-out time.
8. Always leave your room tidy.

Travel Preparations

1. Rule number one for travel is 'Be Prepared'.
2. Make sure that you are well groomed and well dressed, for the way we dress is a symbol of who we are, or what kind of a person we are.
3. If you are travelling overseas, be sure that you have a small amount of local currency at hand.
4. Travel light, ensuring that you do not carry too many clothes and paraphernalia that can be avoided.

5. Carry all necessary documents—passport, visa, driving license, medical prescriptions, inoculation records, tickets, ATM and other credit cards etc.
6. It is always good to draw up an itinerary, and leave a copy of it with someone with whom you hope to be in constant contact.
7. Make use of your travel agent to book all the reservations for the various laps of the journey, car rentals, tour guides, etc.

Public Transportation Etiquettes

Proper etiquette on a bus or train comes naturally to some people, but other just see, oblivious to the people around them. Here are some things to keep in mind when commuting to make the experience more enjoyable for everyone.

Bus Etiquette

1. Avoid loud conversations.
2. Give your seat to an elderly person, a disabled one, or a woman with a child in her arms.
3. Do not talk to the driver while the bus is in motion.

Train Etiquette

1. The basic rules of courtesy as used in airplanes are applicable to train travel as well.
2. Bring blindfolds and earplugs for sleeping.
3. If you want to open or close a window, ask the person next to you if he/she minds.
4. Remember not to litter the floor.
5. Smoke only in designated areas.

6. Keep your children from running up and down the aisles.
7. Do not dump your briefcase and other pieces of luggage on the seat.
8. If you are able—bodied, giving up your seat to the elderly or disabled person is still the civil and decent thing to do.
9. Lend a hand to someone who is struggling to have bags onto an overhead rack.

Auto Etiquette

1. If you are driving, do not take chances while driving, for it is disconcerting to the passengers, and can create tensions.
2. Never smoke in another's car.
3. Do not use cellular phone unless it is absolutely necessary.
4. Park in well-lighted areas.
5. Never stop when waved down by someone standing by a "disabled" car but drive on to the next service station and inform its manager or attendant.
6. Never stop for a hitchhiker.
7. If you are stopped by the police for a driving violation or any other reason, be straightforward and polite, never argumentative.
8. If you are involved in an accident, stay cool, and do not trade accusations with the other driver.
9. If you scrape someone's fender and they are not in the car, do not bolt away, but leave your name and telephone number under a windshield wiper blade.

10. It is polite to offer an older person or the highest ranking person in the group of the passenger seat.

Ship Etiquette

1. While booking reservations on a ship, get a diagram of the ship in advance, so you will know where you are staying—the most expensive accommodations are the larger rooms, higher up and on the outside.
2. Pack light as space is limited on the ship.
3. Address the skipper as Captain and the other officers as Mr., Mrs., or Ms.
4. If the captain invites you to a reception, do not monopolies him in conversation.
5. If you are invited to dine at the captains table—a high honour—be on time and introduce yourself to your dining partners.
6. You may be seated with strangers. If you are unhappy with the arrangement, you may ask the steward to assign you to another one. Do not request seating at an officer's table (that is considered a bestowed honour).
7. Daytime dress in casual, while dinner is generally formal.

Airplane Etiquette

1. Do not show up the airport with arms laden with plastic bags, newspapers, knick-knacks and snacks.
2. Make sure that your luggage tags are secure.
3. Remember that you have to carry your own luggage, either in your hands or in a cart.

4. Make sure you do not stand in the aisle longer than necessary, else you will be holding up other passengers who are waiting to go past you.
5. Keep a watch on your own luggage and do not be quick to agree to watch someone else's luggage you never know what illegal object could be inside, or you may need to move on.
6. Always wait unit all the emergency instructions are announced before you use the earplugs or blindfolds.
7. Reserve an aisle seat if you intend to walk a bit.
8. Do not push the 'call' button unnecessarily.
9. Leave the bathrooms as clean as they were when you entered them.
10. It is polite to ask your neighbour if he/she minds your working on a laptop.
11. Make sure that your telephone calls are kept to an absolute minimum.
12. If a delay mans you have to dash to make a connection, tell the flight attendants before landing, so that they can assist you in deboarding quickly.
13. While leaving the plane, do not get into the aisle until you are ready to proceed toward the door.
14. If there is delay due to a blizzard, a hurricane, a thunderstorm, etc. or you may be provided a reservation on the next possible flight with vouchers for meals and hotel if necessary. Explaining your problem quietly and politely could have a better shot at getting the last seat-if one becomes open—than yelling, threatening and throwing tantrums.

15. When your luggage does not get unloaded after you disembark, report to the airline office for reclaiming the luggage.
16. Always carry your medicines, nightdress, cash, jewellery, toiletries, a change of clothes, etc., in your hand luggage.

    Most importantly just try to always keep in mind that you are not the only person on the bus or train and you need to respect your fellow commuters. Don't do anything the would annoy you if someone else did it.

Other Travel Etiquettes

There may be a whole lot of other people of indefinable category with whom the traveller has to deal. There may be the agents of a product or agency, the sellers of goods, private guides and persons belonging to some such class. There may also be freelancers or interviewers who may be contacting travellers for some information or other. Then there are coolies, gatekeepers, hotel and room attendants. If the traveller is alone, he may have nobody to depend upon unless he can requisition the assistance of the hotel authorities or any other authority which may be under obligation to help tourists. The traveller has to acquire a mature character showing enough confidence during the course of the journey. If he fails in this objective and remains immature and dependent even at the end of all his travels. This confidence should become ingrained in him and he should not try to show off or prove his superiority nor should he sound overconfident or become talkative or too easy for intimacy.

It is his own reasoning that the traveller has to depend on ultimately and he may keep this reasoning clear if he adopts the middle course and behaves neither too showily nor with too much secrecy. He has to maintain a firm but civil tone, and has to examine every proposition and give every proposal his careful thought before acting in accordance with it. One thing which any tourist of reason and good judgment should avoid is a very good or trickle-toffee proposal for any stay, food arrangements or conducted tours, etc. In would be somewhat better to his own. The way of the majority may not be outstanding but it may be the average way replete with all comports and considerations that may be expected commonly. To get the help of some person or persons in whose bonafides he has trust. In the matter tipping also, travelers have to be somewhat cautious and if they tip more or if they do the contrary, both these things may go against them. It is, therefore, necessary for a traveler to get maps, charts and other information, etc about the place from some reliable source before dealing with or engaging the services of others in a new place.

Transporters during Travel

These are part and parcel of any travel, and even of one carries one's suitcase oneself, there are vehicles that one has to hire and on whose honesty one has to depend. It may be unlikely that a tourist has been to the same city twice to know the behaviour-pattern of the transport personnel, and so some amount of natural grit and general courage may be called for. A strong and steady attitude and general alertness may keep off the evil, if there be any, and thus one may depend more on one's practical sense and nature than on any other source.

Cool courage and unruffled calmness any something be more than effective, and even if the worst comes to the worst, one should never lose one's head but should hold one's ground with determination and strength. In all such encounters, weakness in a person is disagreeable to the other person who is to deal with the former.

A traveller who is nervous and panicky form the first and shows his suspicion openly makes it difficult for another to help him and some kind of a row is a possible natural consequence. If, on the other hand, such a person in confident and amiable and engages the other man in pleasant conversation, beings alert and observant at the same time, some sort of liaison or rapport may be established between the traveler and the transporter, and latter may provide best service to the former. Some travellers may treat the driver or the transporter very kindly and in a friendly way. He may treat the latter to all kindly and food and even lunch and dinner that the traveller may be having for himself. Such behaviour, no doubt, endears the traveller to the transporter and in such a sort of good and gracious relationship, the chances of misunderstanding are very few. It is, therefore, through love and friendship that the foreign or any tourist has to win the transporter over to his side because it is naturally advisable to avoid an unpleasant situation or a scene. Certainly, in the face of inevitable evil, the traveler has to put his foot down and take his stand firmly, come what may.

Public Dealing during Travel

This may refer to the etiquette of those who are in charge to travels and tours. The tourist or traveller is generally in search of good advice and it is the public relations people at the airports, at railway stations, at the travel agents' offices to whom the tourist has to turn. Sometime the tourist is experienced and sometimes he is not and it is the responsibility of all these people who are providing service to the public to do so with the greatest of consideration and care. A man at the enquiry counter may have to answer the same questions daily and all the time and yet each time it is new to somebody who may have come distractedly to that counter. If the public relations man realize this and is also sympathetic with the predicaments of those who are in need of advice, correctly and quickly, he may never turn mechanical at his job but give answers wit renewed energy every time.

It is true that the traveller should show patience and fortitude and should not get upset at the smallest inconvenience. Mistakes are sure to occur on both sides but these can be better sorted out and solved with a cool misbehaviour. So the traveller has to be gentle to the officials who may be handling his affairs and with gentleness and tact, a better performance may be extracted than with an adamant attitude of Complaint. Like all public relations men, these men who man the counters and the day-points in travel enhance the prestige of the organization that they work for and if it happens to be the Government, the forging tourist who gets adequate help from a railway guard, a porter or a taxi-driver may remember and bless the country of his visit a ling time afterwards. It is, of course, required that such public relations posts are given to those alone who are experienced, and new personnel may be "positioned only after proper training and a period of apprenticeship".

House Reception

In a house reception, the important thing is the necessary space and if a house does not have such a space which is convenient for the holding of the reception and accommodation all the guests, pandals or construction may be erected adjacent to the house to provide the required space. The welcoming of the guests properly is the first etiquette at a house reception. In this connection it may be added that minor things look magnified in such welcomes. Thus a single smile may be enough to reassure the guest that he is not an unwanted one, while overlooking to do so may start all the secret grumblings and dissatisfactions. Nodding and acknowledgements are necessary and either the host himself or somebody on his behalf should extend these to the invitees. The inmates of the house should know their responsibilities and should branch out in various directions to meet the guests who have assembled under the decorated canopy. They should never together and talk among themselves and look at the guests as outsiders. Each one of the members of the family should take charge of one group at least on his own. The same may be said of the servants of hired bands. They must show mobility and compliance and should know their duties thoroughly. If one has to remonstrate with or take to task one's attendants in front of one's guests, much of the reception-glamour may evaporate.

Even for house receptions, the hour and the duration to the reception may be mentioned on the invitation card, and the guests must keep to this timing or schedule. Because the reception is held at the house and also because the guests happen to be close relatives of the host, it does not give the right to the guests to continue to stay on at the reception far beyond the reception-time. Consideration for the host and the inmates, their fatigue, their inconvenience has to be properly taken note of, and consequently the guests, however friendly they may be with the host, should take themselves off a reasonable hour unless, of course, there is an express request from the host to the guest to stay back linger. The house stands as a symbol of cordiality of the host for the guests and so in house receptions those in charge should be particularly careful since the blame, if any, for ay shortcoming will fall on the host and his party directly.

Public Relations

Public relations happen to be a wide term and may mean all types of contacts with the outside world or circle. Just as the—public relations section in an organization may cater to the needs of publicity and other media to circulate the name and good will of the company, so also at home public relations would give a certain family or household the opportunity to boost its fame and standing in the locality where it is residing. The first requisite of public relations is that the image of the person, body or organization has to be properly projected in the sphere where public relations are being valued and taken up seriously. To get this done in the best possible manner, it is necessary that everybody connected with public relations if fully briefed. If the person giving information hesitates or expresses his doubts or is not sure or is ambiguous, the whole effect of public relations may be lost or neutralized.

To have a trained staff for public relations, therefore is very important. This training has to he rounded up by adequate briefing, so that all the persons disseminating news, facts and information may spell out the same thing and may not be contradictory in their expositions. Politeness is the next requisite of the public relations department. The spirit of help must be inculcated in the persons engaged in this work. If boredom or indifference or impatience and absence of calmness and gentleness become evident, the persons approaching for information may drop out for ever and the company, organization or society may be the loser of the support of a few may be communicated to many, so that the organization gets a bad names for a small lapse such as the telephone operator had replied curtly or some member of the staff had been unwilling to help. The incidents may be insignificant but they proclaim the inefficiency and bad management of the concern. This is because one employee may be inefficient or careless but is the company values discipline, it would order that all of its employees behave courteously according to a common code of conduct. Can we ever imagine a soldier to be it in deficient and still in service without getting the prescribed punishment for inefficiency?

A home or at work, public relations have their place. The good name of an office is necessary for its progress. The good name of the family gives a prop to children in their growing up by supplying a background of respectability and honour. It is a wrong notion that shows of strength is proof of power. Humility has the power to keep hidden a far greater power than can be imagined. In humility and modesty, in good moral character and normal behavior may lie the true seed of courage and grit, a courage that is indomitable and all-pervading. Public relations thus are a major part of public and private life. Unity is strength, the dictator is a freak, and the individualist is indeed a recluse. One can go ahead suppressing others, but not for long. Real advancement occurs only with the acknowledgement, acceptance and acquiescence of all.

Societies

The purpose of a club is mainly to provide relaxation, enjoyment, diversion, etc., while a society may come into being for a particular purpose and it may continue to exist as long as that purpose is present. Thus, the society for prevention of cruelty to animals may find its existence meaningless if Government regulations are passed to safeguard all kinds of animals in the same way as this society would like to go about it to protect animals from human neglect or brutality. In the same manner prohibition societies may cease functioning if drinking is declared illegal. The society to aid flood Victims may still exist even after the victims are provided help and rehabilitated. Such a society may take up some other allied objective to keep itself occupied.

It is needless to say that just like the club a society may have its constitution, its rules and regulation providing for disciplinary action against its erring members. Some societies are actually clubs like a dramatic society or a debating society, while societies like the cooperative credit society, employees, house-building society, etc. are organisational groups existing for the discharge of certain responsibilities or for the implementation of certain objects or ideals. The membership of a society, through there may be compulsory societies like a parent-teacher society in certain schools, or residential welfare societies in a locality where membership is compulsory by virtue of an incumbent being either a parent or a teacher or a resident of the locality, respectively.

It is expected of members that they behave in a mature way and discharge their part of duties in small and big ways. If general meetings are called, members should find time to attend them. If help in cash and kind is repaired, members may do their best to contribute. If other duties are needed to be shouldered, the same may be taken up without much also. Trust and respect among members are necessary. The feeling of hurt, grievance or complaint has to be eschewed. The purpose and objectives of such society are not to be forgotten in the form and formalities, in the different sittings and ceremonies that may be held. Sincerity and sacrifice in members are called for because most of these societies are voluntary welfare bodies. It may not be forgotten by members that pomp ;and splendor are secondary that if a charity show is held in a posh theatre or a modeling exhibition in a five-star hotel, the functions are means to an end, and they are intended to benefit the needy. In these cases involvement in the via-media should not be the only criterion or consideration.

Parents and Etiquette

Children belong to society as a whole and in their proper development, the common action and intention of everybody in society are to be harnessed. Teachers and parents are directly involved in this process. The indifference and apathy of parents with regard to their wards in the matter of education can be considered nothing less than a crime. When a parent gets his child admitted into a good institution and then shuts his eyes completely to his progress, there ate chances that the child may or may not reach the desired standard of achievement. To make it a certainty, the parents have to be intimately involved in the doings and conduct of the child.

The parent-teacher relationship has to be based on a supplementary and complementary assignment. There is no scope for misunderstanding in this. There should be sympathy, mutual help and fellow-feeling. The teacher has to deal with a host of students, sometimes a very large number, and it is understandable that frail as human nature is, mistakes my happen in the teacher's action. It is for the parent to understand the work and burden of the teacher and help him in every way, so that his lack or shortcoming may become apparent to him and he may have the opportunity of retracing his part, the teacher has to keep in mind that the father or the guardian may have other on the next occasion. Oh his part, the teacher has to keep in mind that the father or the guardian may have other responsibilities or he may have a big family, in which case it may not be possible for him to give individual care to every child in his charge.

In these aforementioned circumstances, if there is proper and timely cooperation between the teacher and the parent, they may meet at mutually convenient hours and solve things through discussions. To establish such a teacher not to lower each other in the students' eyes. The parent should build up at home the feeling that the teacher can do no wrong and really no matter what eccentricities a teacher may have, he is capable of contributing. To the growth of students in a major way. Just as patience is required on the parent's part, the teacher has to use extreme tact in dealing with parents. In the ever-growing respect between these two stalwarts in a student's life, the latter's mental faculties blossom in full.

Employee and Worker Etiquette

The employees and the workers who are attached to institutions are also distinguish themselves from their colleagues in other establishments. Institution workers have to cultivate a special kind of zeal and devotion for their work because along with teachers and instructors these workers, like school and college or office employees, have to deal with the young of the new generation in the country and so their responsibility in helping young men and women cannot be belittled. It is common practice in many institutions and particularly with many students that they address members of the office staff of the institution respectfully as 'Sir'. If that be so, the employees have also to treat the members of the young generation of their institutions with due respect and guide or direct them properly.

These aforementioned person should train themselves to acquire the necessary dignity so that starting from the *chowkidar* or the gate-keeper to the office superintendent, all should regard the institution as their very own and should work loyally to improve the level of the students in their organization and take pride in such improvement. This mentality is more important in nurseries and pride in such improvement. This mentality is more important in nurseries and primary school than in places where students are older. But no matter what the ages of the students in the institution may be, everybody in the school should work for strictly maintaining the discipline of the institution. The wrongdoers should be appropriately reported for their misdoings. A great responsibility rests on the gate-keeper of the institution who has been instructed not to let anyone out during school hours. The character or career of many students may be seriously harmed if any lapse occurs in carrying out such orders. Similarly, the office staff may be entrusted with the circulation of important circulars about examinations, tests, tutorials, sports, fees, tours and so on, all of which may have a great bearing on the lives of students. Institutional work requires a great sacrifice and social spirit without which and without the cooperation of the office staff in the institution, the progress of the students may be seriously retarded.

Student Etiquette

It may sound preposterous and meaningless to lay down rules for students when they themselves are to be taught, coached and trained. Yet, there are students of all grades and ages, students belonging to colleges and universities, adult students belonging to institutions and organizations, and in fact among students we may include the whole class of individuals who may be receiving some sort of instruction from others. Barring infants, children and adolescents, the grown-up students should be in the know of the recognized codes of accepted behaviour vis-a-vis those from whom they acquire knowledge.

Students must realize that their teacher may not be perfect and unless they allow the teacher to be normal and concern themselves only with the volume and quality of the education they receive, they may not be able to establish the required relationship between themselves and their preceptor. Anybody who is treated with the teacher's dignity and commands trust and confidence from those who are being taught will naturally be able to give of his best to his students. This art of learning from the teacher is generally known to the intelligent and serious student but it is the average student who creates all the disturbances and may kick up a row about the teacher's alleged incompetence.

Students should remember that in the classroom the teacher is not a person but a teacher and so to indulge in rowdyism, disobedience or to show impertinence and so to harass the teacher is not at all expected of them. They must develop a sense of devotion, purpose adds self-respect and no matter what diversions they may have normally to amuse themselves, these should have nothing to do with their place of study which they should always regard with the greatest awe and respect. They should regard their school as a temple of knowledge. In the same way, respect for teachers is a must for all students. In relation to their teachers, they have to remember the benefits they will receive from the latter.

The Appropriate Dress

We dress for various occasions – attending office, a wedding, dance, party, or just an informal get-together with old friends. Clothes reflect the aspirations and psyche of the wearer. Just as a heavily embroidered saree a picnic would be totally inappropriate, so would minis or jeans be browned upon if worn by a girl when she meets her prospective in-laws or husband-to-be for the first time. The same bright red outfit which looked stunning at a party will be a total misfit at a funeral. A nicely starched kurta-pyjama will look out of place at a business meeting where every other man present is dressed in a suit. Likewise, the same clothes you prefer to wear to office will not do for a formal garden party.

For example, you have recently got married and your husband is happy to escort you around in clothes of you own choice, be it jeans, skirts, etc. But it would be insensitive of you to wear the same clothes when he takes you to meet his old, conservative grandfather for the first time. A saree or even a modest salwer-kameez would be most suited in this instance. In the same way, your husband should not insist on wearing his cut-off jeans or shorts when your relatives come visiting.

This reminds me of an instance. A friend a mine, soon after completing her MA, got a job as a lecturer in a college. She did not give much consideration to what she wore on her first day at college and ended up wearing the first available garment she found – a skirt. The moment she entered the gates, she was accosted by a group of seniors who on mistaking her for a fresher began ragging her. Her protests fell on deaf ears and they thought she was fooling them by saying she was a lecturer. Later, when the truth came out, she was the laughing stock of the whole campus.

Shoes

Indian temple etiquette stipulates that you take off your shoes before entering the premises. The same applies to even certain churches in India. Usually, there will be people stationed outside most temples and gurdwaras, who will keep your shoes safely for a nominal sum. You will be expected to follow the same protocol when you visit as person's home in some of the cities of India. It will, thus, be convenient for you if you wear flip-plops or floaters instead of shoes.

Touching

Indian culture and tradition forbids unnecessary touching contact, especially between a man and a woman, in public. Kissing in public is a not advisable here. You can shake hands with people, or better still stick, to the traditional Namaste, the popular Indian style greeting. For this, you need to press your hands together with all fingers pointing towards the sky in front of your chest and politely say Namaste, while looking at the person you are saying it to.

Avoid Offence

Indian manners and etiquette tips also comprises not speaking ill about or criticise or its people openly. The natives are bound to take great offence to it. At the same time, never address the elderly by their first name, unless they allow you to. It's advisable you call them sir or madam instead. With youngsters, you can choose to be informal. It is also considered disrespectful in India to use strong swear words publicly.

"Social Etiquettes requires only mind and body control it would take some time but it would lead to the best person of the world."

❑❑❑

3
Office Etiquettes

Etiquettes are usually unwritten and generally tend reflect the formulas of conduct in the society. Etiquettes at a workplace are very important. It generally is the key deciding factor in how your colleagues will respond to you and come to your rescue when you require help. Further, the way one conducts themselves in the office with people who eventually become a part of a second family speaks a lot about the kind of person that one is.

Office Manners is about conducting yourself respectfully and courteously in the office or workplace – first impressions are important. Here are some basic office etiquettes that one must follow at a workplace....

Punctuality

Being punctual is very important especially is you have an appointment. It shows that you respect the time of your colleagues and in turn it will compel them to respect your time too. The popular saying that would fit in this situation is that 'Time and tide wait for no one'. Lead by example and everything else will fall into place.

Stay Away from Gossip

Office gossip can make or break someone's career. But it can cause a lot of unnecessary stress which should be avoided at all costs. You would not someone to gossip about you and neither will the next person. In some cases, if the source of some malicious gossip can be traced back to you, then your job can be in jeopardy.

Refrain from being Loud

You must not be loud in the professional work environment, be it while you are on the phone or while talking to a colleague. If you have received a call on your mobile phone then it will be a good idea to walk down to the corridor to take the call. Talking care of this will prove that you respect the work that your colleagues are doing by not disturbing them with your loudness.

Avoid Strong Smells

This may sound strange but a lot of people who work in very small office spaces will be able to appreciate this piece of advice. Avoid using strong perfumes. You can end up suffocation the entire place with your perfume which is closed and the air conditioners usually do not work efficiently. Secondly, some people would also advice you to avoid bring strong smelling lunch like fish to office especially if you are planning to have it at your desk.

Dress Appropriately

Most offices have a predefined dress code that has to be followed very strictly. However, if you do have the privilege of working at a place which does not define a dress code, then it is up to you to dress appropriately. Remember the office is not a party place and you will have to dress in a way that commands respect both from your colleagues and clients. The dress code has a strong influence in establishing the trust that your client places in your abilities in giving them money's worth.

Ask Before Borrowing

If you are at good terms with your colleague then it may appear alright if you borrowed a stapler or a marker from their desk without asking. Well, the fact of the matter is that it is not alright. It is imperative that you ask and then borrow. This attitude of yours will ensure that people also treat your things with the same respect and your things are not missing when you get back to your seat after a meeting.

Your Personal Stationery

1. Even a single-sentence letter can speak volumes about the person sending it, based on the way it looks.
2. A very expensive bond paper letter can be valuable to a friend or relative, but of trivial importance to the person width whom you are seeking a job.
3. A clean paper, crisply folded, and neatly filled with relevant details will speak better in your flavour than costly stationery that is carelessly used.
4. The best statuary is made from rag cottons, but for letter writing, bond paper is the best.
5. A formal writing paper can be engraved or plain, and must be used for things like responding to formal invitations, or for condolence letters.
6. For informal and friendly correspondence, you can use light—coloured paper, or a paper which has a light printed or embossed background.

7. For business, your letterhead can carry the logo, name and address, with email, fax, etc. of the company.

Writing Notes

1. Sometimes it is much easier to write a note to someone expressing your wishes, than to confront the person and say it verbally—here the note can work like magic.
2. While drafting your note, think about who it is meant for—an intimate friend, a person you like someone you have met recently.
3. Also remember the occasion for penning the note—an anniversary, a chance acquaintance, sharing a joy with someone, etc.
4. There are some perennial easy ways to get started while writing a note .e.g. "What a .....(great trip, grand surprise, warm welcome, etc.)" "I was thinking to (or remembering)....." "I can't tell you how much...." "It was so very nice of you to......"
5. A closing to your note should reflect the nature of your relationship with the recipient. e.g. All my love, Best love, Much love, Love, Fondly, Affectionately, Warmly, Regards (in declining order of intimacy).
6. A personal touch is added when you write the note, instead of typing it.

Power of the Pen

1. Plain language is enhanced by simplicity and clarity.
2. Your thoughts and meaning should not be hidden behind jargons and clichés, unfamiliar works and long winding phrases.

3. While writing a personal letter to someone, remember to be candid, making any situation clear, and not indulging in unnecessary details that will produce ennui.

Correspondence

1. Correspondence can be personal or business related, formal or casual.
2. How your correspondence looks is as important as what is says.
3. Correspondence should always follow a pattern, addressing different people differently according to rule and conventions.
4. Letters reveal more of ourselves than we care to think.
5. A letter is a powerful medium of communication, which can be more touching and intimate than even a conversation.

Official Correspondence

Official correspondence bears the stamp of great responsibility which may be easily understood. This responsibility pertains to the fact that an official letter any travel to any authority up and down the ladder of bureaucracy and that action may be taken on the same at the lowest and that action may be taken on the same at the lowest and highest levels. Apart from the fact that an official correspondence has also to be careful about the contents, accusations, stress, avowals, admissions and so on and so forth. When a correspondence is issued officially, the originating source should be prepared for actions taken on it, either favorable or unfavorable, backed even by the ultimate authority, of the requirement be such.

Clarity and brevity are the necessary ingredients of official correspondence. Paragraphs must be devoted to single points mainly, or at best to allied matters. The beginning and the end must be pleasing and should show politeness and form. Economy of words is to be observed, though a certain form of ornamentation at times may be necessary. It has to be remembered that each word in an official letter carries much weight and may be variously interpreted. The writer, therefore, should be careful about the possible significances of words and expressions used in the communication.

Disputes and disagreements are thus the by products of an official correspondence and the issuing source has to take care of all the pros and cons before the communication is despatched. Quickness and pointedness are the virtues reply should be abjured, or corrections or amendments may have to follow simultaneously. Clearness of vision and the spirit of reconciliation, of give-and-take, are the ancillaries that help to solve the matter, and give the needed solution more readily.

Etiquette at Work

1. Maintain a balance between lack of good manners and too much formality.
2. Use the formal style of addressing your seniors – using Mr., Mrs., and Ms.
3. In some workplaces people are quite comfortable with their staff members using their first names-check the norm prevailing there before taking this step.
4. Always keep your conversation brief and to the point.

5. Be ware and wary of malicious gossip in the office.
6. If you hear any malicious gossip that involves you, nip it in the bud by confronting the gossip monger, and politely but firmly setting the record straight with him/her.
7. Offer to help your colleague who is in trouble, only if you are sure you can.
8. One you have helped out someone in dire need, do not go about bragging about it.
9. To maintain perfect harmony with your boss, it is certainly not a sin to flatter him/her and pamper his/her ego, provided it is within limits.
10. Treat all your juniors with grace and respect, and bridge any distance that exists between you, without getting too close to them.
11. While setting disputes between employees, see that you hear the details from both parties before settling it.
12. An office memo should be short, polite and to the point. Avoid flippancy and humour.

Fellowmen

Professionals are, after all, human beings in societies, and apart from their colleagues and customers, there is the whole range of people who surround them, with whom they have to coexist and communicate socially. The professionals' attitude to all these others is important because, besides professional efficiency which may be confined to the court, the clinic or college, they have to give something of themselves to the world. They are human beings essentially and in mixing with their fellowmen, it would be better if they could mix with them on an equal footing and not as experts or superiors.

Also, it cannot be denied that they may be superior to many but this superiority they must never allow to surface. Professionals are the guides, path-finders, social workers, some sort of preceptors, and they have to maintain this dignity and live up to this expectation. What is more, they would blunder if they equate themselves with the common lot. They have to lead the latter, assist them, advise them for self-improvement, even though they are not rendering such help in their professional capacity. Tit-bits of talks, petty imputations, false insinuations should not touch them. Rather, it is they who may be called upon to quell such conflicts between others, just as they would spend their energy in thwarting those directed against themselves.

If this is true, then in their behaviour with their neighbours and fellowmen these experts are not to hammer in their differences. Now would it be right for them to take it for granted that they are accepted automatically. They have to prove themselves as human beings and give expression as to their fellow beings that they are. Not mechanized robots but humans possessed of all the qualities of head and heart.

Opposite Sexes

In the age of women's lib, it is natural that men and women should be working side by side in an office, in a factory and at other place of work. Gone after the days of veils and prudery or false prestige. Women are now going ahead clamouring for equal rights. While glamour, primness and show after attributed to the presence of women in the office, it would also be pertinent to the presence of women in the office, it would also be pertinent to mentions that' one would be mistaken to regard women in such places as only pieces of glamour or extravagance. These working women have their own capabilities and adroitness. These perfection of efficiency, which some of the women can reach in some profession or fields like positions of secretaries, receptionists and so on, may well beyond the comprehension and power of achievement of many a male.

A male colleague, therefore, has to show adequate respect and appreciation for the work that is performed or attended to by the women-members of the staff. Women should be treated as equals and it would be advisable for male colleagues to eat humble pie in their relationship with females in the office. The females colleagues should not be kept excluded from the affairs of the staff in which the male members may take part. If a woman is doing a man-size job, she is entitled to receive a man-size treatment. It is true that in health, haughtiness and physical strength a woman may not sometimes match a man, but that has nothing to do with the quality of work that she is capable of turning out. It would be also wrong on the part of women members to find fault with their male colleagues and maintain fixed opinions about the male sex. It would not be right for women to keep to their shells in the office, or in their own groups. They should have the open mindedness to work with their male colleagues congenially.

Kindness, sympathy, help, fellow-feeling are the attributes of the two sexes as colleagues in the workplace which may create the proper atmosphere of hard and continuous work. Not with standing the different capacities of the sexes, it should not be forgotten that a member may be exhausted in the same manner as the female member at the end of a whole day's work and so in the spirit of camaraderie the small tiffs or the little outbursts, if any, should be withstood by both the sexes. Any form of teasing, banters or unreasonable jokes should be made taboo in an office and unless the employees themselves consciously abandon such behaviour, the standard of the office may possibly suffer.

Visitors

The visitor who walks into an office and expects a red carpet welcome because of his position in the outside world may often meet with frustration and ever humiliation. Every office has its own discipline and its code of conduct. The employer or the manager may be busy with an equally important guest or with a matter or grave concern for the organisation, It may not be possible for him to see the honoured visitors at once without previous notice. The visitors may have to sit outside, generally in the lounge or waiting room provided for this purpose, but it is quite possible in small offices that such a separate place has not been provided in which case the visitor may have to make the best use of a chair at the same table with an employee till the employer or the boss is free to call him inside.

During all this time the visitor's forte would be his smartness, wit and humour. If he frets and fumes, flushes and complains, he may lose his dignity and his mood. He has to be good-natured and find something to talk about with the employee during the period he has to wait. It is for the employee or employees, of course, of offer him some refreshment on behalf of the company and the employer, and be respectfully attentive without neglecting their own work. The more easily an honoured guest can adjust himself to a situation like command from the employees or open appreciation he will employer.

It would also be bad manners for a visitor to turn everything's topsy-turvy in the office or in the parlor simply cause he happens to come from a bigger concern or is a man of a higher status. A visitor has to fit himself in to the structure of the office. If his ultimate objective is to see the chief of the office, he has to use his patience to get over the inconveniences that he may encounter, most of the time inflicted unintentionally. It is also not for him to ask questions or give suggestions or to be too persevering in with his business with the boss, but his dealings outside the boss's office, with the subordinates.

For example:

Visitor – I've an appointment with Mr. K. at ten.

Receptionist – May I have your card, Sir? (takes the card). Could you please wait for a few moments? Please make yourself comfortable (pointing to the sitting arrangements in the room and indicating a seat to him). Then after contacting the concerned person, Receptionist—I am very sorry but something has come up. Mr. K. will be free in five minutes. Could you please wait for a few minutes?

Visitor – Certainly, I'll wait, I quite understand.

Colleagues

In an office, in reality, all persons are colleagues. The work is before them, they have to do their respective duties to deliver the goods jointly. The master and the servant, the superior and the subordinate may have bureaucratic differences but actually such differences are meaning less. As a colleague in the working force in an office, a person should treat another colleague with dignity and politeness. There is no room for snobbishness or for complexes. Noble birth, good education, possession of wealth has no value if a person is unable to perform the work allotted to him. His working efficiency is the first and foremost requirement in the office and he has to be respectful to all those who are engaged in bringing out efficiency in full to the surface.

Colleagues should not be placed on the same footing as friends. Certainly colleagues may become, in course of time, the greatest of friends but behaviour proper to friend may not be ordinarily proper to a colleague, friends may be normally of the same age and status, but this is not the case with colleagues who may be of different ages and come from different strata of society. In the office if there is any difference, it may exist only in respect of work and nothing else. An old gentleman has to show appropriate respect to a young person if the latter happens to be doing the same work as himself. Pride, aloofness and indifference are to be absolutely cast off among colleagues, or the work of the organization will suffer. In proper coexistence and fellow-feeling, one should learn the art of working together with one's colleagues. The office is not the place for giving vent to one's emotions. People may laugh and talk and joke and even discuss family matters but work should have priority. As long as a colleague is capable, he is entitled to all the respect and attention, irrespective of their conditions such as his appearance, his status, and his finances and so on.

Employers

In the business and service world, superiors may very well be employers, but they are not always the same. A superior may be any one of the intermediaries who has the responsibility of managing or manning the office or a particular department. The employer, on the other hand, would commonly mean the highest or chief person in the organization who has not only the power to give employment but also to relieve a person of the job, if need be. Employers, therefore, as a rule would not have any superiors unless, of course, we take into consideration all the customers and clients or members of the governmental authorities to whom the employer has to be indirectly indebted, responsible or obliged.

The relationship between the employer and the employee is not that of the cat and the dog. On the contrary, since a person has to employ or a person has to serve in one form or another, this relationship should be mature and sensible. It is a fact that if a person has to go ahead in his working life, he has to give his best to his employer. It is also true that an employer may get a number of persons in his employment but he may find difficulty in getting really efficient and devoted persons to work for him for any continued length of time. If that be so, the employer is just as much indebted to this loyal employee as the latter is to the employer. In short, workers there may be many and to spare but good and sincere workers are very few indeed.

If an employer considers his employee inferior, he would be committing a serious blunder. He pays his employee a salary in return for his work. He has to be considerate and kind to him. The employee cannot contribute his maximum to his work if he cannot rely on his employer at times of crises. Employees are not a herd of dumb-driven cattle. They are the implements of production of wealth for the country. Only through cajoling and sympathy "can the highest amount of efficiency be got out of them and that too with their cooperation". In a work-place where the employer is able to create the right type of cooperation and a feeling of mutual trust and friendship, the total efficiency may be automatically maximized.

It does not cost the employer anything to address the employees politely. There is, however, no hard and fast rule and the employer who generates in his employees strong bonds and works shoulder to shoulder with them may be permitted even to deal roughly with the latter who may rather like it since they may admire or worship their boss. This boss has to be the moral master and not simply the physical or circumstantial one. If the boss loses his temper, if he is inconsiderate, hard to please, revengeful and so on, he can never be a true master to his employees. In the face of contingencies and chaos, it is the master who has to take charge and command and lead his team. If, on the other hand, he raves and shouts and is nervous and frantic, his employees will have scant respect for him. He is the employer, he is taking all the risks, and he has to shoulder the entire burden.

Subordinates at Office

Though superiors are there to order and manage, the work of the subordinates is no less important. The peon who cleans the master's table, the typist who types the letters for him and the driver who is attentive to his duties throughout the day and at time even at night are the most useful people in his working life. The work of the organization may come to a standstill if all these small, big and medium pillars of action do not function in a coordinated manner. Work is sacred and today's subordinate may have the possibility of becoming tomorrow's master. Despair and frustration are evils that eat into a subordinate's efficiency and have to be discouraged and dispelled.

The important thing for the subordinate is to remember his place, the range of his duties and his limitations. Orders are to be carried out without question and the subordinate who fits himself into this operational and the will automatically catch the eye of his master or at least will never go unnoticed. To know one's duties and to obey orders may not be so easy in the practical field, as it may appear in theory. There may be contingencies where the subordinate may have to use his own intelligence, or make decisions on his own. There is no doubt that these are small decisions but they are decisions all the same, and the subordinate who has taken the correct step once may go ahead in life following in that step.

There are curtsies, bows and so on that a subordinate has to extend to his superiors in the office. It is also customary for a subordinate to stand up and dip standing when the boss is at his table. But rules differ from office to office and while some offices may be strict in this respect, others may do away with such formalities. The absence of formalities, however, should not do away with the form. Talking and speaking come next to gestures. A subordinate must learn to hold his tongue when the superior has taken over the discussion and unless he has to point out any outstanding misdirection, he better be silent.

Superiors

The relativity of the official status of the superior and the subordinate is amazing to anyone not initiated in laws of the working world. There may be practically nobody who may be superior or inferior as such, because the same person may be superior to one and inferior to another, and so on the process goes backward and forward, upward and downward, and hence in the office almost everyone has to be conscious about the rights and duties that fall to his share other as a superior and as a subordinate. The main objective of an office is to produce something or superiors have their exalted positions with much bigger responsibilities which they must discharge to best benefit of their office or concern.

It is true that superiors in the office enjoy better facilities and amenities but their burden is also greater and to retain their position successfully, they should not only be efficient and hardworking but should also possess the necessary tact, generosity, compassion and so on. Let us take the chief man in an office, the manager, for instance. The manager has multifarious responsibilities. He has to take care of those under him; he has to maintain proper good will and relationship with outsiders, customers and so on; he has to see the administration and efficiently of the case may be, besides shoulding innumerable other duties which are unclassified.

The manager has to be general, soft, permissive, strict, vigorous, reserved, good-humored, pliable and inflexible, as occasion demands, to those working under him. A manager cannot turn a deafer to the appeals and entreaties of other employees. He cannot throttle the spirit of progress or block efficiency of his subordinates. He has to inspire cooperation, not extract it. He has to provide scope and the right atmosphere for development for those who are loyal and deserving. He has to have personal knowledge of his staff and know how to get the best out of them. Civility is an asset to him, at the same time he cannot allow himself to be slack in his behaviour. He has to be gentle with the sensitive and overbearing with those who are rough and rugged. But he should not bear any grudge, should keep himself from getting involved in their affairs, personally or emotionally, either adversely or intimately, and should keep his head above the common surge.

How to Dress for Office Party

Keep one thing in mind. Never wear attire that will make you the topic for hot gossip after the party. If something about your clothes does not seem right, then it probably isn't. You need to make heads turn when you enter and then slowly fade away with the backdrop. It is not advisable to be in the limelight forever! Choose your attire according to your party venue, occasion and the invitation.

Pick something that is dressier than what you would wear to office on a casual Friday. The idea is to pick something that is causal & smart and yet pulls you through like a professional. In case you need to go to the party venue from work, get the dress or a part of it along with you in a bag.

Consider what kind of a party is it going to be. If it requires you to stand for a long time or dance, avoid short dress or short skirts. If it an evening cocktail party, don't wear bright colours and instead stick with darker colours with sheen and shimmer. The best bet would be to team a neat looking pair of jeans that has sequins around the pocket, with a sexy shirt. In colours like white, liver, ivory, copper, rust, hues of blue, etc. It could be a sleeveless number or a nice halter neck. Make sure it doesn't flaunt too much of cleavage and your midriff is covered. Accessorise with a black, brown or white jewelry. It could be a neat pair of chandelier earrings or a chunky metallic bangle or a thin necklace.

If the theme is mentioned in the invitation, stick to it. A cocktail party normally calls for a short black dress but don't go for something that is too short. If it is dinner party, consider wearing formal trousers and a dressy shirt.

Guys can always wear formal to semi-formal trousers with no creases and a dressy shirt. Ties are always optional and the shoes have to be neat and polished. Get a black or brown blazer to go with your attire and gel up your hair. Don't forget to shave off your stubble and you are set to rock!

New Workplace Etiquettes

1. **Forget the exit interview.**

   An exit interview won't help you, and it'll probably create bad will. If you have people to thank when you leave a job, do it at lunch. If you have ideas for how to improve the company, offer to consult. Of course the company will decline, because they don't care. Otherwise you wouldn't be quitting right make sure that parting ways goes as smoothly as possible so that you can shepherd this person into your network of supporters.

2. **Don't ask for time off, just take it.**

   When you need to leave work for a few hours or a few days, you don't need to ask for permission—you're an adult, after all. Make sure your work is in good order and send an email to the relevant people letting them know you'll be gone.

   This will seem discourteous to older people, who expect you to ask rather than tell. So be sure to give a reason why you're cutting out. People like to know the matter and where they stand.

Cell Phone Etiquette in the Workplace

Having your cell phone at work can be useful but it can also be very disruptive. Your friends and family can reach you anytime, anywhere, which can be annoying. Here are some rules you should follow if your have cell phone at work.

1. **Turn your cell phone ringer off.**

   If you have your cell phone at work, it shouldn't ring. If you don't want to turn off your cell phone completely, at least set it to vibrate. The sounds of different ring tones going of all the time can be very annoying to others. In addition, you don't want your boss to know how often you get calls.

2. **Use your cell phone only for important calls.**

   If you have your cell phone at work, you should only use it for important calls. What should you classify as an important call? The school nurse calling to say your child is ill, your child calling to say he's arrived home from school safely, and family emergencies that you must deal with immediately are important. Your friend calling to chat, your child calling to say dog had an accident, or your mom calling to tell you your cousin is engaged should not be considered important.

3. **Let your cell phone calls go to voice mail.**

   While you are at work if you are in doubt about whether an incoming call is important, let voice mail pick it up. It will take much less time to check your messages than it will to answer the call and then tell the caller you can't talk.

4. **Find a Private place to make cell phone calls.**

   While it's okay to use your cell phone at work for private calls during breaks, don't stay at your desk. Find somewhere else to talk, where your conversation can't personal. You may be on a break but your coworkers have a job to do.

5. **Don't bring your cell phone into the restroom ever.**

   This rule should apply to using your cell phone at work or anywhere. Why? Well, if you must ask-you never know who's in there; the person on the other end of the line will hear bathroom sounds, e.g., toilets flushing; it is an invasion of your co-workers' privacy.

6. **Don't bring your cell phone to meetings.**

   Even if you have your cell phone set to vibrate, if you receive call you will be temped to wee who it's from. This is not only rude, it is a clear signal to your boss that your mind isn't 100 percent on your job. All calls can wait until your meeting is over or until there is a break. Remember, there was a time before we had cell phones.

Office E-mail

Make the subject line specific. Think of the many messages you're received with the generic subject line, "Hi" or "Just for you".

Don't forward massages with the three pages of mail-to information before they get to the content. In the message you forward, delete the extraneous information such as the entire Memo to, "subject, addresses, and date lines."

When replying to a question, copy only the question into your e-mail, then provide your response. You needn't hit reply automatically, but don't send a bare message that only reads, "Yes." It's too blunt and confuses the reader.

Address and sign your e-mails. Although this is include in the To and From sections, remember that you're communicating with a person, not a computer.

DON'T TYPE IN ALL CAPS. IT'S TOO INTENSE, and you appear too lazy to type properly. This is still a written medium. Follow standard writing guidelines as a professional courtesy.

Some Dos and Don'ts

Here's a list of dos and don't that may help you understand the parameters within which you must work.

What you must not do

- Don't try and find 'best friend' among your colleagues.
- Don't try and get up, close and personal with your boss.
- Don't try and seek audience from the next cubicle when talking on the phone.

- Don't keep ringtones of your mobile very loud when at work.
- Don't peep over colleague's shoulders to read their emails.
- Don't entertain jokes that have sexual overtones.
- Don't comment on people's sense of dressing.
- Don't try and seek unnecessary attention by constantly talking about your achievements.

What you must do

- Do reply to office mails and try to use lower cases while typing as bold letters signify a scream.
- Do keep you voice low while talking.
- If you have a problem that may force you to stay away from work, keep your boss in the loop.
- Do congratulate a colleague on his/her achievements ever if you do not approve of his/her ways.
- Do not forget to shut you mobile phone during meeting.
- These are some etiquettes that you can follow in a professional work environment. However, it is more important or ensures that to behave decently and courteously, if you treat people in the way that you would like them to treat you, then it is more than half the battle won and people usually end up respecting to equally.

❑❑❑

4
Telephone Etiquettes

We've all heard about them from the time we were very young—manners, manners, manners. Mothers all over the globe do what they can to instill some kind of proper etiquette in their children and many succeed. However, when many people use the telephone etiquette seems to disappear. Not only that, but it isn't uncommon for someone to experience poor business and they don't use proper telephone etiquettes, the businesses will most likely loose customers. Talking on the telephone is no different than speaking with someone in person, but for some reason a piece of electronic equipment between the mouth and the ear tends to make people forget that there is such a thing as phone etiquette.

One of the most common situations where we immediately forget any kind of telephone etiquette is when a salesperson calls on the phone. Our initial reaction is that the telephone call is unsolicited and unwanted. Why should we be polite to a business person that is interrupting our personal time with an uninvited phone call? Well we wouldn't verbally assault the perfume sample dispenser in a department store, but they are doing the same thing the person on the phone is doing-selling product. The person on the phone is just as human and deserves to be treated with courtesy. Not to mention it is far easier to simply say "No, thank you" and "Good-bye" than getting worked up and feeling guilty later on.

Since many to us seem to have forgotten telephone etiquettes, here are a few telephone etiquette tips as an update to skills that are quite natural in many of us. Always answer the phone by saying, "Hello" and not any other greeting. If the person who has been requested is not available, simply state that he or she "is not available at this time. May I take a message?" Not only does the person on the other end of the phone have a good impression about you, that feeling will apply to the person they are calling for as well.

Always be quick and to the point while remaining pleasant during a phone call. Friends and family will continue with a telephone conversation if they have time, otherwise they are not likely to rush you off of the phone no matter how busy they are. No one is perfect, so if you dial a wrong phone number state your mistake, apologize and hang up the phone.

Businesses are beginning to realize that without providing telephone etiquette training, many employees are offending or even angering customers on the phone. New hires are often presented with a guide for telephone etiquette and some may even have to go to professional telephone etiquette training. Proper phone etiquette is important at both a personal and professional level. Being polite on the telephone is just as important as when speaking with someone in person. You might be surprised at how good you feel about yourself if you use proper telephone etiquette and the positive responses received while talking on the phone.

Cell Phone Etiquette

With the numerous technological advancements today, one of the biggest blessings to the field of communication is the cell phone. You feel so much at ease when you know that you can contact or update your loved ones about your whereabouts or seek help in an emergency. However, as there are exceptions to ever scenario, cell phones tend to become a nuisance for the majority, when an individual misuses it or is unaware of the basic 'etiquette'.

Cell phone etiquette comprises of a few simple guidelines of following common courtesy when using a cell phone in public, designed to make public places enjoyable for all. It is important to understand that the general public is not interested in your private conversations, arguments, details, official business meetings or intimate information that is loudly discussed on your cell phone. For the benefit of every cell phone user, here are a few ground rules that spell 'cell phone etiquette'.

Keep it Short and Sweet

When you are in a public place like a shopping mall, theatre restaurant or even an elevator, keep your conversations brief. You can get back to the caller when you are in a private space and where your conversation does not disturb the people around you. When you are watching a movie in a theatre with hundreds of other people, make it a point to switch off your cell phone and deep it in silent mode. Movie goers do not buy tickets to be disturbed by loud cell phone users. Remember the cell phones should to switched off in movie theatre, playhouses, or any other public place that creates an atmosphere to elevate the imagination of the audience. People pay good money to be entertained, not for something that spoils the illusion.

Multitasking is Not a Good Idea!

Refrain from talking on your cell phone while driving. Multitasking on the road can be dangerous and can lead to accidents. Didn't we all survive without the cell phone a few years back? If anything urgent, upsetting or distracting, stoop the car and pull over to a corner of the road and speak. Do not talk and drive simultaneously. By doing that you are risking the lives of many other people on the road while risking your own too.

Follow Common Courtesies

Turn-off your phone before a job interview, presentations, official meetings or boardroom meetings. Leave it off at funerals, weddings or any place where a quiet atmosphere is mandated such as a courthouse, museum, library, place of worship or any public venues. It is a question of being considerate and to empathies with other's needs and convenience as well. When it so happens that you need to answer an important call, ask the people around you "Do you mind if I make a call?" or "Can I answer this?"

Public Places

Intimate public gatherings such as restaurants, public restrooms, waiting rooms, hallways, buses, subways are all places where a private conversation is not possible. In such places when you are forced to stand close to others they are also forced to overhear your private conversations. At such times, you can practice good cell phone etiquette. You can put the ringer on silent or vibrate mode or let the call roll over to the voice mail. Alternately, if it is an important call that you must take, step outside or into a secluded area to return the call.

Speak Softly

Many cell phone users tend to speak loudly. Little do they realise that there is microphone in the gadget that is perfectly capable of hearing normal voice tone. When you are not shout over the phone interrupting everyone around you. You may appear rude and uncouth to the onlookers. Get up and move to a secluded place or exit to the back hall to receive the signal or to make calls. At times, when you are not aware that you are loud, take your cue from the response of those around you. If the connection is bad, tell the caller that you will call back when you find a spot with better coverage. Short text messages (SMS) in silence are ideal in such situations.

Basic Cell Phone Etiquette Rules Include:

1. **Switching it off –**

   Know when to turn it off or vibrate it. e.g. meetings movies, worship, seminars, etc. vibrate mode when in places where you can take a call, but don't want to disturb others.

2. **Be Brief –**

   When you get a call and you're with friends, keep the call short.

3. **Permission –**

   Often, it is correct etiquette to inform other at the beginning of the meeting that you are expecting an important call and get their permission.

4. **Be polite -**

   Don't scream: speak in a lower-than-normal voice, you will be heard by the caller, and not others in the room.

5. **Don't Distract -**

   Avoid talking where you may be distracting to others.

6. **Driving -**

   It is not only very dangerous, but also unlawful in most countries (even India) to drive and talk on your cell phone

Cell phone etiquette is essentially about being considerate of others and to remain empathetic and conscious to other's needs as well as convenience.

Business Telephone Etiquettes

The telephone has become an indispensable tool in businesses today. Cell phone technology is rapidly changing. It is imperative to know all the rules while talking on a phone for business purposes. Business telephone etiquettes should be taught to all members of the organisation. This will leave a good impression of your organisation on both the callers and the called.

When you pick up the phone, greet the person depending on the time of the day. While calling you should introduce yourself and give the name of your organisation if you are working in one. Use short phrases and simple worlds while talking on the phone. Long-winding sentences will lead to disinterest and poor comprehension in listeners. Avoid the use of casual words and slang. Sales people could call you. It is not compulsory to hear out an entire sales pitch. One can ask the salesperson's name and business and politely express disinterest in the business or products. Further you can request your number to be removed from the calling list.

Proper customer service is an integral part of business telephone etiquettes. There should be screening of calls by possibly the receptionist before forwarding it to the voice message on the phone if the person is not able to take the call at the particular time. If the phone gets disconnected due to some reasons then instead of waiting for the call, callback the person right away. You should avoid multitasking like handling different phone calls at on time. There should be proper scripts for inbound and outbound calls.

If you dial a number that is wrong, apologize promptly and disconnect. One ought to dial carefully and in proper lighting to avoid calling a wrong number and causing inconvenience to others. Etiquette demands that both the caller and receiver should write down information when required. Before making a call or taking one, be sure to have something to write upon. In case the conversation is confidential you should speak from a private room where no one else is present. In case this option is not available speak softly and at the volume not audible to neighbouring colleagues. Ideally you should not put a person on hold. You ought to ask permission before putting the person on hold. Unauthorised persons should not be permitted to use the phone. This may have a detrimental effect on the reputation of your organisation.

You should never eat food or chew gum while talking on the phone. It causes unpleasant sounds and could possibly irritate the user. Do not talk on the phone while driving. This is not only dangerous but will also divide your attention. Speak softly. Make sure volume of the phone is not very high as well as speech should be able to be distinctly heard. The correct way to answer the telephone is 'hello'. Simply answering "yes" is an inappropriate and terse response.

You should never be rude to a caller no matter whatever provocation business like manner. Speak clearly and slowly when talking a business call. You should not mumble or have slurred speech. Keep phone calls brief and friendly. You ought to be mindful of different time zones. Try to call during the day as far as possible. Calls before 9 am and after 9 p.m. should be avoided. You should also be careful in calls where cultural difference come by complimentary words and phrases may be considered derogatory in other cultures.

Most Frequent Caller Complaints

Remember that presentation is everything. Treat callers as you would hope they would treat you. The way you present yourself on the phone can leave lasting impressions of you and your department.

1. **"The telephone rings for a long time before it is answered."**

   Try to answer calls within 3 rings. Callers become frustrated when they feel that their call is not important to you.

2. **"The place me on hold for sometimes, it seems, houses".**

If you find yourself placing many calls on hold, write down the name of the caller and a brief description of what they are calling about. If the caller has been holding for quite a while and know they will be holding even longer, pick up the line and say: "I'm sorry, but the person you want to speak to/need to speak to is still unavailable. Did you want to continue to hold or would you like me to take a message/send you to their voicemail?"

3. **"The line is busy for hours it seems."**

   Try to keep calls short. Do not stay on the line longer than is absolutely necessary. Consider call waiting for you personal office (not for a receptionist) so that you are not constantly unavailable.

4. **"They are very rude and get offensive when asked their full name or sometimes just won't give it."**

   Try to stay pleasant. Callers are not trying to be rube be asking your full name. often, student will be given incorrect information and then are asked: "who told you that?" if all they know is that "Jane" gave them the information, it will be difficult to track down the person who gave out the incorrect information.

5. **"They let me talk on and on only to realise that they're not the person I should be talking to."**

   Politely interrupt the caller if you are unable to help them. Don't waste your time (and theirs) by listening to a long story and then transferring them. Say "Excuse me, sir/mam but I am unable to assist you with this issue. Let me transfer you to Rakesh who will be able to assist you." If transferring them to another department, indicate that you are doing so. If you are not sure who can help them, place them on hold and ask someone in your office. If no one is sure, tell the caller "Thanks you for holding. Unfortunately, I'm not sure who would be able to assist you with that. Let me transfer you to the campus operator and perhaps they can assist you.

6. **"If I call the wrong department for help, they don't give me suggestions to where I should be calling, they just say, 'I don't know, not our department."**

   Frequently, you will find that your number is similar to another department on campus. Rather than hanging up on a caller or saying you don't know, try to be helpful (within reason). If you have the time, ask someone in your office if they happen to know who help the caller. If you do not have the time or can't find the answer, say "Unfortunately, I am not sure who can help you with this problem. Let me transfer you to the campus operator and they may be able to assist you. "Try to find out the answer to these frequently asked questions (or finger out which department's number is similar to your own). Wouldn't you like the Sales Department to transfer you to the Service Department if you incorrectly dialed their number?

7. **"They don't clearly listen to my needs before they transfer me to the wrong person."**

   Listen to the caller carefully! Before transferring them, be sure you understand what the caller wants. Repeat what they said back to them. "Let me be sure that I understand you situation. You requested a transcript and would like to know if it has been sent. Is that correct?" This gives the caller a chance to clarify his/her situation. You may receive many calls about the same issue, but treat each caller as an individual and don't jump to conclusions.

8. **"Sometimes they disconnect me while transferring my call."**

   Be careful when transferring a call. Sometimes accidents happen, but be mindful especially during high volume times. In order to transfer, first tell the caller where you are transferring them. Second, press the Xfer button. Dial the extension where you are transferring the call. Press the Xfer button again.

9. **"They told me to call back, but never gave me a number or division to ask for."**

   If you tell a caller to call back later, tell them which number to call. Even if you give them the main department number instead of your personal extension, it will help if they were transferred to you by another department. Tell them who to call and give them an approximate time to call back. (i.e. "Ms. Rosy is unavailable right now. But if you call 278-2011 in about an hour and ask to speak to her, she should be able to take your call.")

10. **"The person says, 'wait' and then talks to other coworkers without putting me on hold so that I can't hear their small talk."**

    Use the hold button! Whenever you are going to leave a caller to check something or to help someone else, use the hold button. Callers shouldn't hear the background noise of your office even if it will be for a short while. If what a caller hears is different from what you tell them, they may be confused or angry.

11. **"They answer with an aggravated voice, as if I disturbed them by calling".**

Remember that students are the reason there is a university. It is difficult to stay polite all the time, especially during the high volume periods. But again, your disposition reflects on the campus and your department. Try to treat each caller as you would hope to be treated.

However, customers are ones who become the main source of income into a business, they do not tolerate being treated with rudeness in their dealings with a company. This includes any business that is conducted on the telephone. The telephone is our link to the outside would. Unfortunately, we don't always realise what kind of message we are sending to our callers. Therefore, here are tips for Business Telephone Etiquette.

Answering Calls for your Department

1. Answer promptly (before the third ring if possible).
2. Before picking up the receiver, discontinue any other conversation or activity such as eating, chewing gum, typing, etc. that can be heard by the calling party.
3. Speak clearly and distinctly in a pleasant tone of voice.
4. Remember that you may be the first and only contact a person may have with your department, and that first impression will stay with the caller long after the call is completed.

5. Use hold button when leaving the lines so that the caller does not accidentally hear conversations being held nearby.
6. When transferring a call, be sure to explain to the caller that you are doing so and where you are transferring them.
7. If the caller has reached the wrong department, be courteous. Sometimes they have been transferred all over campus with a simple question. If possible, attempt to find out where they should call/to whom they should speak. They will greatly appreciate it.
8. When the called party is not in, the following responses should be used both to protect the privacy of the office staff and to give a more tactful response:

What you mean:	**Tell the caller**
"He is out."	"He is not in the office at the moment. Would you like to leave a message on his voicemail?"
"I don't know where he is."	"He has stepped out of the office. Would you like to leave a message on his voicemail?
"He is in the men's room."	"He has stepped out of the office. Would you like to message on his voicemail?"
"He hasn't come in yet."	"I expect him shortly. Would you like to leave a message on his voicemail?"
"She took the day off."	"She is out of the office for the day. Can someone else help you or would you like her voicemail?"
"He doesn't want to be disturbed."	"He is unavailable at the movement. Would you like to leave a message on his voicemail?"
"She is busy"	"She is unavailable at the moment. Would you like to leave a message on her voicemail?"

Voicemail Etiquette

Voicemail has many benefits and advantages when used properly. However, you should not hide behind voicemail. If callers constantly reach your voicemail instead of you, they will suspect that you are avoiding calls. Here are a few tips on such things as greetings and responding to voicemail.

Voicemail Greeting

1. Be sure to record your own personal greeting: don't use the standard default greeting or have another person record your greeting. People tend to feel that they have already lost the personal communication touch because of voicemail. If a female voice says that "Vimal is not available", the caller will not be convinced that you listen to your voicemail.
2. Write down what you want to say in your greeting and practice saying it a few times before recording. Even if the greeting sounds like you are reading it, it will ensure that you don't spend as much time trying to record it "just right."
3. Include in your greeting your name and department so that people know they have reached the correct person.
4. Your regular greeting should include your normal work hours. If you know that you will be on vacation for a few days or leaving the office early or have different hours temporarily, you should record an alternate greeting to let callers know this. Callers will know that they cannot expect a callback for a few hours or a few days.

5. Use the attendant feature! This feature allows the caller to reach another person in your department from your voicemail. For example, if you were out of the office on a Thursday and a caller needed an answer immediately, the caller could dial 03 while listening to your voicemail message and be transferred to someone else in your department. You have to select an attendant yourself-it is NOT done automatically. Try to select someone who would know your schedule and be able to take messages for you—such as a receptionist or assistant. To find out how to select an attendant, see the voicemail Guide which is available at the Telephone Services website.
6. If your phone is the main department extension, you might want to consider playing an alternate greeting when you are closed.
7. If your message is rather long, you might consider informing callers of the option of press 5 to by pass your message and to start recording their message to you.
8. If you on the paging feature (you will be paged when a message is marked urgent), make sure to mention that in your massage. Callers leave a message and then press 4 to mark the message urgent. You will be paged with 2525 to let you know that you have an urgent voicemail. To set-up the paging feature, contact Telephone Services.
9. When you leave for the day or will be away from your desk for an extended period of time, forward your line to your voicemail using the call forward feature as a courtesy to your callers. Call forwarding means that

your callers don't have to wait through an entire ring cycle before leaving a voicemail message for you.

Checking Messages and Returning Calls

1. Check your messages daily and return messages within 24 hours. If it will take linger than 24 hours, call the person and advise him/her. Callers should feel comfortable that you are checking your voicemail daily.
2. Reply, forward, or delete massages immediately. Keep your mailbox clean. Saved messages kept longer than a week take up needle space in your mailbox since you are only allowed 20 messages total in your mailbox, including saved messages.
3. If you forward a message, be sure to explain to the person to whom you are forwarding the message why you are sending it to them.

Leaving a Voicemail Message for Another Person

1. Speak clearly and slowly.
2. Be sure to leave your name and extension number. It's best to say it at the beginning and end of your message.
3. Keep message short and to the point.
4. Remember that you want to leave the person you are calling with a good impression of you.
5. Leave the date and time you called in the message. Let the person know the best time to call you back.
6. cover one topic in one message; specify what you want the recipient to do.

Voicemail Defaults

1. Maximum greeting length=90 seconds.
2. Maximum message length the someone can leave in your voicemail box=3 minutes.
3. Maximum number of messages that can be lift in your voicemail box=20
4. Maximum number of days that messages are kept (messages that you have not listened to)=90 days.

Transferring Calls

To transfer a call:

1. Let the caller know where you are transferring them.
2. Press Xfer
3. Dial the extension where you are transferring them. (i.e. 2300 for Admission and Records)
4. Press Xfer again. You're done.

To announce a call:

1. Find out the name of the caller and ask what it is in regard to. (Why they are calling)
2. Tell the caller to please hold for a moment.
3. Press Xfer.
4. Dial the extension of the person the caller wants to speak to. (i.e. x9999 for Vimal)
5. Wait for the person to answer.
6. Tell the person (i.e. Vimal) who is calling.
7. *(a)* if the person accepts the call, press Xfer.

(b) if the p·rson asks you to take a message, press RLSE (release), then press the button where the caller is holding. From there you can take a paper message or transfer directly to a person's voicemail.

To Transfer a Call Directly to Voicemail (without ringing):

1. Tell the caller you are transferring them to (name's) voicemail.
2. Press Xfer
3. Dial x6525.
4. Dial the extension of the person you are transferring them to (i.e. Vimal at x9999)
5. Press the # key and then Xfer.

Note: Once you hit the # key, the voicemail message starts almost immediately. So in order for the caller to her the entire message. It is important to press the Xfer key soon after hitting the # key.

Good Telephone Procedures

Remember that you are representing your department and etiquette is very important. Using phrases such as "thank you" and "please" area essential in displaying a professional atmosphere. Here are some useful points for telephone procedure:

Make Sure to Answer before the Third Ring

Examples of greetings can be: "Telephone Services, may I help you?" OR "Good morning" ...you get the idea. Use a greeting that is going to give the caller the impression that we are in fact professional and pleasant.

If you are Currently on one line and another line rings:

1. Tell the first caller to "Please hold."
2. Place caller on hold.
3. Answer the ringing line saying, "[Department name]
4. Place second called on hold.
5. Return of first caller and complete the call.
6. Go back to the second caller.
7. Say, "Thank you for holding, may I help you?"

Note: Sometimes you will have many lines ringing all at once. Please remember to write down the names of the calls holding so you avoid asking who the called is holding for more than once. Follow the above steps, placing as may calls on hold as necessary.

Screening Calls

Answer the phone by saying: [Department name], how may I help you?"

1. If the caller asks to speak to the dean (for example), ask "May I tell him/her who is calling?"
   - Ask the caller "What is this in regard to ?" (If appropriate)
   - Press Xfer and the extension.
   - Wait for the dean to answer.
   - Announce the name of the caller.
   - Wait for a response as to whether the call will be taken.
2. If the called party wishes to take the call, press the Xfer button again.

3. If the calling party does not wish to take the call, press the RLSE button and then the button where the caller is. Say: "__________is out of the office, may I take a message or would you lime his/her voicemail?"

Taking Message

1. Be prepared with pen and message slip when you answer the phone.
2. When taking messages be sure to ask for:
   - Caller's name (asking the caller for correct spelling.)
   - Caller's phone number and/or extension (including area code)
   - If the caller is a student, ask for the student ID# (If appropriate) and ask what the call is in regard to.
3. Repeat the message to the caller.
4. Be sure to fill in the date, time and your initials.
5. Place the message slip in the called party's inbox or in a conspicuous place in their chair.
6. Don't forget that you can transfer them to voicemail instead of taking a paper message, but don't forget of ask, "Would you like me to transfer you to _____'s voicemail?" Do not assume that the caller would rather go to voicemail. Always ask first.

Handling Rude or Impatient Callers

1. Stay calm. Try to remain diplomatic and polite. Getting angry will only make them angrier.
2. Always show willingness to resolve the problem or conflict.

3. Try to think like the caller. Remember, their problems and concerns are important.
4. Non-supervisory: Offer to have your supervisor talk to the caller of call him/her back if the caller persists.
5. Supervisor: Be willing to handle irate callers. Speak slowly and calmly. Be firm with your answers, but understanding. Sometimes the irate caller just wants someone in a supervisory capacity to listen to their story even if you are unable to help them.

How to End Conversations Gracefully

There are several way that you can end a long phone call without making up a story or sounding rude:

1. Leave the conversation
2. Promise to finish your discussion at another time.
3. End on an "up" note.
4. Tell the person how much you've enjoyed speaking with him/her.

As long as you are honest and polite with the other person, you shouldn't have any problems getting off the phone and onto something else.

Finally following good business telephone is the responsibility of every person in the organization. These are simple and effective but inexpensive methods to enhance the image of your organization.

❑❑❑

5
Manners

A manner is a particular way of behaving or doing something. In sociology, manners are the unforced standard of conduct which show the actor to be cultured, polite, and refined. They are like lawn in that they codify or set a standard for human behaviour, but they are unlike lawn in that there is no formal system for punishing transgressions, other than social disapproval. They are a kind of norm. What is considered "mannerly" is highly susceptible to change with time, geographical location, social stratum, occasion, and other factors. That manners matter is evidenced by the fact that large books have been written on the subject, advice columns frequently deal with questions of mannerly behavior, and the schools have existed for the sole purpose of teaching manners. A lady is a term frequently used for a woman who follows proper manners; the term gentleman is used as a male counterpart; though these terms are also often used for members of a particular social class. Here are two points including in manners that is:

Social Grace

Social grace are skills used to interact politely in social situations. They include manners, etiquette (the specific accepted rule within a culture for the application of universal manners), Deportment and fashion. These skills were once taught to young. Women a a finishing school or charm school. They focus of social grace has changed over the last century. Recently with an emphasis on business etiquette and international protocol.

Politeness

Politeness is best expressed as the practical application of good manners or etiquette. It is a culturally defined phenomenon, and what is considered polite in one culture can often be quite rude or simply strange in another.

While the goal of politeness is to make all of the parties relaxed and comfortable with one another, these culturally defined standards at times may be manipulated to inflict shame on a designated party.

The British social anthropologists Penelope Brown and Stephen Levinson identified two kinds of politeness, deriving from Erving Goffman's concept of face:

1. **Negative politeness:** Making a request less infringing, such as "If you don't mind..." or "if it isn't too much trouble..."; respects a person's right to act freely. In other words, deference. There is a greater use of indirect speech acts.

2. **Positive politeness:** Seeks to establish a positive relationship between parties; respects a person's need to be liked and understood. Direct speech acts, swearing and flouting Grice's maxims can be considered aspects of positive politeness because:

   - they show an awareness that the relationship is strong enough to cope with what would normally be considered impolite (in the popular understanding of the term);

- they articulate an awareness of the other person's values, which fulfils the person's desire to be accepted.

Some cultures seem to prefer one of these kinds of politeness over the other. In this way politeness is culturally-bound.

The Importance of Manners

Manners are the un-enforced standards of conduct which show a person to be cultured, polite and refined. They set a standard for human behaviour. What is considered to be "mannerly" is highly susceptible to change with time, geographic location, social stratum, occasion and other matters. Manners matter is evinced by the fact that large books have been written on the subject and that schools. Have existed for the sole purpose of teaching manners. A good manner is the first mark of good breeding and reflects directly on a person's upbringing; therefore learning good manners begins at home and should be taught by parents. Good manners do not come naturally, they have to be learnt if children were not told and shown how to behave politely they will grow up rough and rude like savages. Manners are something used every day to make a good impression on others and to feel good about one – self. Good manners are more than "opening doors" and "writing thank you notes". While opening doors for others and writing notes is nice, true courtesy goes deeper. Being polite and courteous means considering how others are feeling. If we practice good manners, we are showing people around us that we are considerate of their feelings and respectful. We are also setting standards for other's behaviour and encouraging them to treat us with similar respect. "Treat others the way you want them to treat you". Good manners are not the same in all countries as different nations have different customs. In England it is a mark of respect to take your hat off in another persons house or when you meet people you know in a street, but in India it is polite to keep the hat on and rude to take it off. However, good manners may be different in different places, the principle of good manners is always the same everywhere—it is consideration for the feelings of other. Good manners are very important as they teach us the way to behave in society. They enable us to make favourable impression on others, in school, at job interviews, in business and in just about every situation in life. Children who understand and practice good manners feel more self—confident and become more proactive in their dealings with adults. This feeling for self-confidence is very important for our future success.

Manners make a person to look different from the other. Today parent is very conscious about to teach Good manners to their children. Here are some tips to make good and well-mannered.

Good Manners

Good manners occupy a unique place in our life. They are to be acquired and cultivated. The sooner it is done the better. Childhood is the best period for learning and imbibing good manners. The Bible says, "Train up a child in the way he should go and when he is old enough he will never depart from it." It is obvious that is in the formative years that good conduct, behaviour and manners are to be developed and cultivated.

As old says, "The childhood shows the man as morning shows the day". Thus manners must be emphasized from childhood.

Good manners are the sure keys to success. They are not only social behaviour but also an ideal form of personal conduct and character. There are little courtesies that make the machine of life run smoothly. They are valuable possessions. They help in making friends, winning over people and in gaining appreciation and admiration. Propriety is the basis of all ethics. Manners make men and morals.

In business and service they are indispensable. They help us avoid better and untoward situations. We should never fail to say sorry if we disturb people. Even in our personal and private lives they are important assets. It is good manners to thank people for a service, guidance or a gift received.

To be late for appointment and keep people waiting is indiscipline. To respect elders, to greet them or to give them precedence is always good behaviour.

Good manners reflect how properly cultured, civilized and social enlightenment. They reflect refinement and social enlightenment. They make a lasting and favourable impression on people. Without good manners man is nothing better than an animal or barbarian.

They are to be developed and imitated. Bad manners bring a bad name to the school as well family. Hence proper emphasis should be laid on learning good manners in the very early days of life.

The best way to educate hildren learn from observation. Learning manners is like learning a new language or a musical instrument. It is very easy to learn something in childhood. So start planting seeds as young as possible. The foundation of good manners can be strong in your age.

In good manners, cleanliness is also important. Put the habit of hygiene from very early stage. Here are tips for inculcating the value of cleanliness in children.

1. **Start with the room**

   Put a habit to keep the things in the right place. Set down certain parameters. For example, a child should never be allowed to use dirty hankies or towels. Never allow the child to bring the shoes on the bed, however tired he or she may be.

2. **The next step is the bathroom**

   We should teach our children to brush their teeth, clean their bottoms and have a nice bath. They must also learn to keep their surrounding clean. For example, you could put up a funny little poster that reminds your son to pull the flush. Or put up a little bell that rings every time he forgets to shut the door.

   Teach you children to conserve water by shutting the all taps in the house as well. Be it in the bathroom or kitchen, or anywhere under the sun.

3. **What about other places?**

   In order to maintain cleanliness, never allow your children to eat in any place of the house. Teach your children to lay the table neatly. Make sure that both your son and daughter pick up their own used plates and carry them to the kitchen sink. They should also offer to carry those of the aged members of the family. Washing their hands and gargling after meals is also a very good habit, as it will help them fight bad odour throughout life.

4. **Cleanliness at public places**

   Encourage your children to apply the same cleanliness standards in the public and private too. You have to ensure that you children do not litter a park when on a picnic or that they do not throw garbage from a running bus/train.

Helping Children with Manners

Manners are constantly changing from one century or one generation to the next. For example, a handshake originally was meant to show that men were not carrying a sword or dagger in their hands. Men still tip their hats because once knights in amour lifted the visors of their helmets to show their face. And it wasn't too many years ago that a man almost always got up in crowded bus and gave his seat to a woman. Nevertheless, certain manners do survive from one decade to the next, and this is because manners make life easier for everybody.

There are three important ideas behind the good manners we use today: custom, consideration, and common sense. Custom is the habit of doing certain things like shaking hands and tipping hats mentioned above. Consideration is the most important idea behind all good manners. Almost always, beings well–mannered. Consideration is simply thinking about the way the other person feels. Being rude to someone is a bad manner, not because a book says so, but because it causes hurt feelings. Nearly all good manners have in element of common sense. If you are standing in the rear of a crowded elevator, it's neither reasonable-nor good manners-to try pushing your way to the front so you can get out first.

These are the basic ideas we want to teach our children when we are trying to instill good manner—simple kindness, consideration, and common sense. The following suggestions written for and directed to children may give some added authority in the matter of what is common courtesy and what is not.

Manners at Home

Home is where you learn to get along with people. 'Me closer you live with other people, the more important good manners are. Everybody in a household should respect the right and feelings of everybody else. Try to listen when others in the family have something to say. Even a little brother or sister who can't yet read or a grandmother who seems quite old has a right to an opinion.

It is important for members of a family to consider each other's privacy. No matter how crowded a home is, everyone in it has a right to some place that is his own. Here are some privacy don'ts.

1. Don't open a closed door until you have knocked and waited for permission to enter.
2. Don't go into anyone else's bureau, desk, box, or papers at home or anywhere else without his permission.

3. Don't read anyone's mail or anything he has written (for example, a diary) unless he asks you to.
4. Don't discuss the private affairs of your family with outsiders or tell about a family problem.

Another important part of family good manners is sharing. You share the TV set and the telephone and the bathroom and maybe a bedroom or a closet or a desk. You share the work. This mean cleaning up after you and sharing the responsibility for the safety of everyone in the house.

Being a Guest

We all know that we have certain responsibilities when we are the host or hostess. But there are responsibilities when one is a guest that are equally important. Here are a few of them:

1. Don't go visiting unless you're expected.
2. Don't overstay your invitation.
3. Don't expect to be waited on. Offer to help.
4. Don't plan to stay overnight without consulting the hostess and your parents.
5. Don't upset the family's routine. Try to fit in and your part.
6. Don't make extra work. Make bed, straighten up after yourself.
7. Be sure to say thank you for a meal or an overnight visit at a friend's house.

Table Manners

These suggestions below are good manners to practice at home.

1. Wash your hands before sitting down.
2. Leave toys, book, and pets behind.
3. When you sit down, place the napkin in your lap.
4. Sit up straight and don't slouch.
5. Ask politely for dishes to be passed. Never reach across the table.
6. Wait until everyone is seated and served before starting to eat. It grace is said, wait to eat until it is completed. Don't giggle during grace.
7. Keep your elbows off the table.
8. Never chew with your mouth open.
9. Never talk with a mouth full of food.
10. Use utensils quietly without banging them on the table or plate. You should place your knife softly on the edge of the plate when not in use.
11. Slice butter from the butter dish and place it on your butter plate or other plate. The butter knife should stay with the butter dish.
12. Never wave or throw utensils.
13. Keep your knife out of your mouth.
14. Never play with your food.
15. Never grab food from other people's plates.
16. Ask politely for seconds if you want them.
17. Ask to be excused from the table.
18. Clear your plate from the table and take it into the kitchen.

Remember, good manners are important and make meals more enjoyable. You will be proud if you learn these rules at home. Then when you go out to eat, they will be habit.

Telephone Manners

Always give the person you are calling plenty of time to get to the phone before you hang up. If the person who answers is not the one you want, give your name and ask if you may speak to the person you've called. Ask, "May I speak to Romy?" not "Is Romy home!" If he isn't in, you may leave a message.

If someone dials your number accidentally, accept his apology. Everyone sometimes dials a wrong number. No one intends to. If you accidentally dial a wrong number, excuse yourself.

It is considerate to make phone calls at a time when they will not disturb people. Try not call too early in the morning (before about 9:00) or too late at night (after about 9:30). Try not to call at mealtime.

It's handy to keep a pencil and paper near the phone if someone calls a member of the family who is not at home, ask the caller if he would like to leave a message. If he does, be sure to get his name and number. If you take a message, be sure to remember to deliver it!

Office Manners

Office Etiquettes or Office Manners is about conducting yourself respectfully and courteously in the office or workplace-first impressions are important. Here are some tips:

1. Always act with honesty and dignity. Chewing gum and popping bubble gum in the presence of co-workers is neither cool nor dignified. Never do it whilst attending customers.
2. Wear appropriate office, for example correct footwear, not thongs (flip flops) – they are strictly casual or beachwear.
3. No exposed midriff to display tattoos and body piercing. Be neat, clean and as conservative as the business requires you to be.
4. We are put off by smell people. So, be sure to shower regularly and use a suitable deodorant.
5. Do not cough or sneeze in anyone's directions. Use a tissue, if possible, to contain the germs and then say "Excuse me".
6. The essence of good manners and etiquette is to be respectful and courteous at all times and with everybody.
7. Therefore, treat your co-workers, people and others with respect and courtesy.
8. Good office etiquette is easily achieved by using common courtesy as a matter of course.
9. Keep your interruptions of others to a minimum and always apologies if your intrusions is an interruption of a discussion, someone's concentration or other activity.
10. Show respect for each others workspace. Knock before entering.

11. Show appreciation for the slightest courtesies extended to you.
12. Be helpful and co-operative with each other.
13. Brush up on your computer skills so that you can help others.
14. Speak clearly without shouting. Loud people are a vexation.
15. Say, "Please; Thank you; You're welcome", as part of your everyday courtesy.
16. Be discreet and compassionate in your criticism of a co-worker.
17. Don't gossip about any co-worker's private life.
18. Do not try to sell things to your colleagues.
19. Don't hover around while waiting for a co-worker to get off the phone. Leave a note for them to call you or return later.
20. It's not a good idea to take your iPod to your office. It hinders communication.
21. Avoid sexist comments about a co-worker's dress or appearance.
22. Surveys show that the office know-it-all proved to be the biggest gripe amongst co-workers. Don't be a know-all.
23. Take responsibility for your mistakes, apologies and go about correcting it.
24. Apologies if you are clearly in the wrong. If in doubt, apologies anyway. It's no big deal.
25. Never blame someone else if it is your mistake.

Manners on the Street

Unless you are at home or at a friend's house, you are on public property. Because this property is used by many people, it is especially important that everyone use common sense and good manners. Here are some street don'ts:

1. Don't walk in bunches of that you block others.
2. Don't stop to chat in the middle of the sidewalk. Step to the side so that people won't have to move around you.
3. Don't stare at or make fun of anyone, on matter how strange he may look.
4. Don't be a litterbug.
5. Don't mark on buildings or other public property.
6. If you bump into someone or step on his toe, say you're sorry.

Corporate Manners for Freshers

Every day new and young faces from professional and arts colleges make their entry to corporate services. Many of them accomplish themselves as successful entrepreneurs and outwit their counterparts to reach high positions. On the other hand the left group of freshers may wonder where they have failed in the race despite their proven calibre. Here are some corporate manners for freshers that would definitely add more competence to their calibre.

1. Always enquire about the timing of arrival, departure and breaks if, you are not informed beforehand.
2. Follow Golden Rule in a corporate "Never Be Late."

3. Your dressing is an expression of your attitude. Enquire about the company dress code or simply observe your would be colleagues. Dress positively to boost your impression.
4. Express a warm greeting to the receptionist whenever you pass her/him. He/She knows everyone at office and would help you to build office relationships.
5. Learn the office layout from the receptionist through casual talks.
6. You can find somebody in your team who you can rely upon and seek help from them during emergency cases.
7. Maintain a proper sitting posture.
8. Never personalise your cubical with family photos and other little accessories.
9. Keep your personal call to the lowest possible number (Read it as Zero) during the first few weeks. In addition keep the ringer volume low yet audible to you.
10. Do not use office e-mail or surf the internet for personal purpose.
11. Try to solve your duties rationally and never depend too much on others.
12. Never postpone your duties to the next day.
13. Be willing to extra duties or help your colleagues. However more importantly, know when you have to say the word "no".

14. During lunch time ask your colleagues to join you or go to the lunch room for food. This will enable you to interact with people from other departments too.

15. Never give out too much personal information about yourself to everyone. At the same time never be too inquisitive and gossip about others.

16. Always update yourself with knowledge of business and competition by reading journals, watching programmes, discussions etc.

17. During the first meetings and presentations share ideas but, keep your opinions to yourself.

18. Always keep eye contact with others while talking.

Let these corporate manners take you to new heights of your career.

"The golden rule for manners is to feel the importance of treating others. So stress the importance of treating others in the same way they would lime to be treated."

❑❑❑

6
Dining Etiquettes

There are a number of Dining Etiquettes irrespective of culture and tradition. But Dining Etiquettes vary from one country to another. They even vary from one religion to another A general knowledge and use of basic etiquette makes the dining experience more pleasant for everyone. The rules of etiquette have been set—up for a reason-to give people a guideline for behaving in a manner that will make those around you comfortable. A command of basic table manners and dining etiquette is especially useful for dinner meetings, an evening in an exclusive restaurant, and at formal affairs. Acquaint yourself with the following guidelines and dine with confidence.

Formal Dining Etiquettes

In these time of fast food, it has become imperative to brush up our formal dining etiquette. Now-a-days, formal sit–down dinners are becoming less frequent. There comes a business lunch or a dinner at a swanky restaurant where you are required to be sophistication incarnate displaying flawless table etiquette.

Behaving boorishly on that one important dinner due to a lack of adequate knowledge of table manners could be your undoing. It is not difficult to pick up the basics. So let us brush up our table manners.

In any invitation, there are two perspectives. You are either the host or a guest. The main table manners, however are the same in both cases.

Let us have a look at some of the common table manners.

1. It is perfectly okay to eat finger foods with your fingers. You can bite off pieces of larger savories. If they are messy, use your fork or spoon, the following items – bread, cookies, corn on the cob, chips, French fries, sandwiches, small fruits, berries, and cubed cheese are finger foods.
2. Never put an entire sandwich, however tiny, into your mouth. Eat it in small bites.
3. Take care not to dip the serving tongs into your teacup while adding sugar.
4. After stirring sugar into your tea, place your teaspoon on the saucer.
5. Never blow on your tea. A hot cup of tea should be kept on the table to cool off. And don't slurp when you drink anything.
6. As soon as you are seated, pull out the napkin from its setting, unfold it and place it on your lap. Never truck

napkin into your collar. At the end of the meal, allow the waiter to clear all your plates. Then lay the napkin at the centre of the table.

7. If you have to leave the table inadvertently during the meal, put your napkin on the left of your plate or leave it on your chair with the soiled part facing down.

8. If you happen to drop napkin on the floor, do not pick it up. Signal to the serving staff to supply you with a fresh one.

9. Dab your napkin lightly on your lips. Never scrub your mouth with your napkin.

10. Do not stretches across the table to pick up politely ask the person nearest to it to pass the item to you? If you are requested to pass something, pick up and place it near the person next to you. Things are not passed hand to-hand. In addition, it is incorrect for anyone other than the original requestor to use the item passed.

11. Never talk with your mouth full of food. Cover your mouth if you need to cough or sneeze.

12. Do not rest your elbows on the table. It is okay to put part of your upper arm on the table.

13. If you have something in your mouth that you want to spit out, put it on the fork and place in on your plate discretely.

14. The correct way of using a spoon or a fork is by balancing them between the first knuckle of the middle finger and the tip of the index finger while using the thumb to steady the handle. The knife if used with the

tip of the index finger gently pressing out over the top of the blade.

15. Hold the fork with your left hand spoon (or knife) with your right. However, you can dispense with the spoon (or knife) if you use the fork, How held your right hand.
16. To indicate that you have finished your meal, place the fork and knife (or spoon) horizontally on the plate, parallel to each other, facing away from you.
17. To drink your soup, half fill your soup spoon and moving it away from your body sip it from the side of the spoon.
18. When presented with the finger bowl, delicately dip your fingers in the water and gently dad them with the napkin.
19. It is inappropriate to ask for a doggy bag when you are a guest. Save the doggy bag for informal dining situations.
20. It is best to order foods that can be eaten with a knife and fork. Finger foods can by messy and are best left for informal dining.
21. Do not order alcoholic beverages. Drinking too much when dining out is one of the most disliked behaviours.
22. Do not smoke while dining out.
23. Sit up straight at the table. It makes a good impression.
24. When you are eating, keep your hand on your lap or resting on the table (with wrists on the edge of the

table). Elbows on the table are acceptable only between courses, not while you are eating.

25. Do not season your food before you have tasted it.
26. Never chew with your mouth open or make loud noises when you eat. Although it is possible to talk with a small piece of food in your mouth, do not talk with your mouth full.
27. Do not slurp soup from a spoon. Spoon the soup away from you when you take it out of the bowl and sip it from the side of the spoon. If your soup is too hot to drink, let is sit until it cools; do not blow on it.
28. If food gets caught between your teeth and you can't remove it with your tongue, leave the table and go to a mirror where you can remove the food from your teeth in private.
29. Eat rolls or bread by tearing off small bite size pieces and buttering only the piece you are preparing to eat. When ready for another piece, repeat the same process.
30. Engage in table conversation that is pleasant but entirely free of controversial subjects.
31. You should not leave the table during the meal except in an emergency. If you must go to the bathroom or if you suddenly become sick, simply excuse yourself. Later you can apologise to the host by saying that you didn't feel well.
32. If you need something that you cannot reach easily, politely ask the person closest to the item you need to pass it to you. For example, "After you have used

them yourself, would you please pass me the salt and pepper?"

33. If a piece of your silverware falls onto the floor, pick it up if you can reach it and let the server know you need a clean one. If you cannot reach, it tell the serve you dropped a piece of your silverware and ask for a clean one.
34. If you or someone you are dining with is left handed, it is best for the left-handed person to sit at the left end to the table or at the head of the table. This arrangement helps ensure that everyone has adequate elbowroom to eat comfortably.
35. If food spills off you may pick it up with a piece of your silverware and place it on the edge of your plate.
36. When invited to a dinner, arrive on time and leave on time. Do not wait till the host starts dropping not-so-subtle hints like "what a big day I have tomorrow." Many a times you decide to invite a prestigious guest for a meal at a high-end restaurant. The person is important to you. There are certain do's and dont's, if followed diligently, would leave a favourable impression on your guest.

There are a few things you must ensure to make the occasion a resounding success.

1. Choose a restaurant conducive to your meeting. Keep in mind the taste and profile of the guests and the occasion before selecting the place. If you are meeting to discuss something important, give the restobar a miss. Opt for a muted, classy place instead.

2. Make reservations in advance. It would be unseemly to land there and find no place. If you have visited the restaurant before, book a table suitable for your meeting.
3. Inform your guest about the venue and time and confirm that the reservations have been made under your name.
4. Always reach the place 10 minutes before the appointed time. Check whether everything's is in order.
5. Inform your waiter that are waiting for someone and request the waiter to direct him or her to your table on arrival. It would to direct him or her to your table on arrival. It would be a good thing to find out the waiter's name.
6. While waiting, you can order a non-alcoholic beverage for yourself.
7. Have a look at the menu and find out the specialities of the day.
8. Do not talk about personal issues while the waiter is present. Once he has taken the order and moved away, draw your guest out with small talk on general topics like the water or the guest's interests etc.
9. Offer the menu to your guest. Give your suggestions regarding the options only when asked.
10. Turn your cell phone on vibrator mode.

Be it at a restaurant or home, a formal dinner requires a formal dress. You are expected to dress for the party. At the end of the, your self-confidence carries you through.

Serving Food

1. Pass food from the left to the right.
2. If asked for the salt or pepper, pass both together.
3. Food is served from the left.
4. Dishes are removed from the right.
5. Butter, spreads, or dips should be transferred from the serving dish to your plate before spreading or eating.

Tripping Etiquette

At a restaurant, always leave a tips can very from 15% to 25%.

1. Waiter: 15% to 20% of the bill for extraordinary service.
2. Wine steward: 15% of wine bill.
3. Bartender: 10% - 15% wine bill.

Toasting Blunders

1. If you are being toasted, sit there calmly, and thank your host later.
2. If you have toast, do not read from any paper. Let it be either extempore, or commit it to memory.
3. Do not make your toast long; let it be short and apt.
4. If you are the guest of honour, do toast the host in return, either soon after the host has toasted, or during dessert.
5. Do not tap the rim of your glass to get everyone's attention.
6. If you are a teetotaler, make a toast with any other soft drink, for it is the thought that counts.

7. You can toast for more than one person, for example, a whole team or an entire family.
8. Do not pre-empt, but allow the host to be the first one to toast.

Use of Cutlery

1. When you use a fork and spoon, the former is held in the hand while latter is held in the right hand.
2. While using a knife and fork also, the fork is in the left hand, while the right hand is used for the knife for cutting.
3. At a sit-down meal, generally two pieces of cutlery are used at a time, though the other pieces are also laid out on the table.

Eating Gracefully

1. You can eat cake with the fingers if it is bite-sized, otherwise use the fork and spoon, with the spoon in your right hand for scooping it up.
2. When you squeeze a lime between the fingers, use the other hand to shield the lime squirt so that the diner beside you is not subjected to an eyeful of lemon juice.
3. Oranges and sweet limes can be peeled with a knife, and each segment of the fruit eaten with fingers.
4. When pineapple is cut into pieces, use a spoon, else, use a fork.
5. While eating a watermelon, use a spoon. Put the seeds into the palm of your hand, and transfer them to the side of your plate.

6. Pasta, spaghetti or noodles should be eaten with a fork, twirling or coiling a few stand the fork before eating them.

7. Food served on plantain leaves in South India requires eating with fingers.

8. Use a fork and knife for a dosa or anuthappam, with the knife in the right hand.

9. When idli or vada is served, use a spoon. First eat a small piece of idli, followed by a spoonful of chutney or sambbar.

10. Rice is generally eaten, using a fork and spoon.

11. Use your finger to break papads into tiny bits as you eat.

12. Use your fingers while eating any kind of leavened bread, roti, chapatti, nan, puri, etc.

13. Dry vegetables can be eaten, using a fork, while the gravied ones require a spoon.

14. Kababs and cutlets are eaten using a fork and knife.

15. If you are served large pieces or a whole wedge of lettuce, cut one bite at a time, using the knife provided. If the salad is served before or after the main course, use the smaller fork. If the salad is considered the main course, use the entrée fork.

16. Small pieces of boneless chicken can be eaten, using a fork. You can also use a knife.

17. Chicken with bones, or tandoori chicken are best eaten, using a fork and knife. Be careful while handling the greasy pieces.

18. Fish is generally eaten, using a fork and knife.
19. Cut the spring rolls into bite-sizes and use a fork to put them into your mouth.
20. Burgers, hotdogs and patties can be eaten, using your fingers.
21. Small sandwiches, such as tea sandwiches or canapés, may be picked up and eaten with your fingers. Large sandwiches, if not cut in halve, should be cut with your knife before lifting and eating. Any hot sandwich served with a gravy requires a knife and fork.
22. Use a knife and fork to eat fresh pineapple slices.
23. Pizzas can be eaten, either using the fingers, or a fork.
24. Chips are eaten with the fingers and French fries with a fork. Never pick up the whole piece and bite part of it off.
25. For pav bhaji, use a knife and fork for the bread and a spoon for the vegetables.
26. Salads can be eaten, using a knife or fork.
27. Pastry can be eaten with fingers, or a fork and spoon.
28. When an omelette is served with toast, use a knife and fork, else use only a fork.
29. Sandwiches are easily handled by fingers.
30. Do not slurp while having soup.
31. Dessert can be eaten, using a dessertspoon or a small spoon, or even a fork, depending on the sweet served.
32. If you are resting between meals. Cross your cutlery the fork on top with prongs facing down.

Buffet Etiquettes

Buffet can be real etiquette challenges with a long queue of people often tackling a limited supply of food. It is a cost effective and quick way to serve meals to large numbers and hence, extremely popular at corporate events and in restaurants. While buffets may seem like a free-for-all, the rules of etiquette still apply. Keep these tips in mind the next time you're at a buffet to eat your fill but with politeness.

1. **Queuing**

   Queues at a buffet can be annoying, as everyone wants to serve themselves first but do politely wait your turn instead of sneaking up to the counter. Wait for the food to be replenished instead of scraping the dishes. Eating while waiting your turn or serving is avoidable behaviours.

   Buffets serve large numbers and are not to be compared with the experience associated with fine dining in a sit-down meal. While standing in the queue, stop complaining about the food or caterer or the long wait as it is impolite to the host. Instead use this time to network or chat with the others waiting with you.

2. **Serving**

   Use the serving spoon or tongs to serve yourself and not your fingers Resist the urge to pop that papad directly into your mouth, on matter how tempting it looks. One serving spoon per dish is provided and should be replaced on the holder or back in the dish.

   Avoid accidents and spillages by bringing your plate close to the serving dish. When deciding what to eat, don't sniff the food, instead take a small amount and return if you like it. For hygiene and safety purposes, avoid leaning over the dishes while serving yourself.

Avoid sampling all dishes and over-loading your plate. Instead, exercise choice and serve limited portions of select dishes, such that the food is neatly arranged on your plate.

3. **Going for Seconds**

   A second round to the buffet table is usually expected, but a third is not. It is typically best to use a fresh plate for your second round. Remember, a buffet is a completely self-service meal so don't ask the servers to clear your plate or get you a second helping. Do so yourself and then enquire about where you should discard your plate.

4. **Buffet Courtesies**

   Buffet are self-serve meals but the buffet counter staff needs to be thanked if they serve you. The clearance staffs have an extremely tough job and need to be thanked when taking away the used plate from you.

Tea Party Etiquette

1. Since it is a tea party, it's okay to eat with fingers. However, if an item is particularly messy (has a runny filling like a pastry), then use a fork.
2. If all courses are laid out on the table, eat them in this order: first the scones or muffins; then the tiny sandwiches, and last the sweets. Think of it like a meal where you can start with bread, then have the main course, but save the dessert for last.

3. For scones or muffins, break off a bit-size piece, then put it into your mouth.
4. Take bites of the tiny sandwiches. Never stuff the whole things in their mouth, even though it's small.
5. If using sugar, be careful to not dip the sugar tong or sugar spoon into the tea.
6. If the tea is hot, do not blow on the tea. Leave your teacup on the table to cool.
7. Do not stick your little finger out when drinking tea just hold the teacup normally.
8. If there are tea bags, then make sure to place or use a small dish on which the used tea bag can be placed.

Dinner Etiquette

1. Place Plate – the place plate is placed one inch from the edge of the table. If the first course is already on the place plate, the napkin is placed to the left of the fork, otherwise the napkin will be on the plate.
2. Forks/Flatware – Handles of the flatware are aligned at the bottom. The forks (no more than three) are at the left of the place plate, placed in order of use, working from the outside in. The oyster fork is the only fork on the right side with the knives, tines of the fork placed upward, across the soup spoon or parallel with the knives.
3. The salad fork is positioned the furthest from the plate on the left. One would use this fork first. In the case of French style dining, the salad would be served after the main course. In this case, the salad fork would be positioned next to the plate.

4. Knives – Knives, no more than three, are at the right of the place plate in order of use, from the outside in, with the cutting edge toward the plate. The only spoon (for a first course) is placed to the right of the knives.
5. Dessert Silverware – The dessert fork and spoon are above the place plate, the bowl of the spoon facing left, the fork below facing right. In the most formal setting, the dessert fork and spoon are brought in on the dessert plate.
6. Glassware – No more than four glasses are set on the table, in order of use, for water, white wine, red wine and champagne, from the left to the right.
7. When filling glasses don't overfill!
8. Stemware – Note the shapes of each type of stemware. They all have a unique shape and should only be used for their respective drinks.
9. Bread and Butter Dish – The butter plate (optional) has the knife placed across the top of the plate, handle to the right, edge of blade toward the user. The salt and pepper are above the place plate, pepper to the left of salt. Large salts and peppers to be shared are placed slightly below the wine glasses and between everyday two place settings.
10. At the end of the meal, you should place your used silverware close together on the plate, with the utensils entirely on the plate (less than an inch of the silverware over the side of the plate). This is a signal to the servers that your meal is finished and the dishes can be removed.

11. For a formal dessert service, a waiter brings each guest a finger bowl filled with water. The bowl is set on a small lace or organdy doily (optional), which in turn sits on the dessert plate. The dessert fork and spoon are balanced on the plate in this case (instead of sitting at the top of the place setting throughout the meal). A guest should dip finger tips in the finger bowl, wipe them on his or her napkin, and then remove the finger bowl and doily to the upper left of the place setting. He or she now moves the fork and spoon from the plate to the left and right of the plate respectively. The empty plate is now ready to receive a helping of dessert.

Napkin use at a Private Dinner Party

The meal begins when the host or hostess unfolds his or her napkin. This is your signal to do the same. Place your napkin on your lap, completely unfolded if it is a small luncheon napkin or in half, lengthwise, if it is a large dinner napkin. Do not shake it open.

The napkin rests on the lap till the end of the meal. Place the napkin in loose folds to the left of your plate.

The host will signal the end of the meal by placing his or her napkin on the table. Once the meal is over, you too should place your napkin neatly on the table to the left of your dinner plate. (Do not refold your napkin, but don't wad it up, either).

Cocktails

Cocktails generally are more homely affairs than receptions. It is needless to say that in cocktails, wines and spirits may be served along with other assortments of soft and cold drinks. Snacks are also provided at cocktails, the main objective to which is to meet guests and get acquainted with them. In informal cocktails, the guests may wear what is suitable for them according to the fashion of the day. The cocktail is normally for the duration of about an hour and a half, though this period may be extended a little, depending on the convenience of the host and the guests. It is evident that conversation and the art of mixing are the soul of a cocktail party. Since cocktail parties are to be small, there may not be place for all the friends and acquaintances that a person would like to please by inviting them all to one.

The ideal number at a cocktail party may be round about ten, a little more or a little less than that. The guests should bring out their best to mix with one another. However, the guests that are invited are to be mainly regarded as those of the host concerned and other guests normally should not pick up friendships or become intimate with any of them unless they also meet in the business or working world. This rule, however, is not applicable at bigger receptions where friendships may be freely picked up and then cocktail invitations dispatched to get closer to one another. Discussions of a general nature are ordinarily the rule at cocktails but there is no harm if the talk moves on to more specified subjects and some sort of semi-business discussions ensure.

It is common courtesy to return a cocktail invitation, that is, give in return a cocktail invitation to the host who had earlier invited you. But, it is not always necessary that the guests and the hosts become so intimate as to continue to reciprocate this kind of invitation. Where strong drinks or liquors are served, it is necessary for the gusts to keep their heads and not become drunk so as not to be able to take care of themselves. In this connection a person should know how for he is capable of standing drinks and this limit should not be crossed, for that would cause embarrassment to the host since the party is usually small and compact. Too much boisterousness which may go unnoticed at a reception will not be in place in a cocktail party of a moderate size.

How to open a Champagne Bottle

Make sure the champagne is cold: Start off by chilling the bottle. The best serving temperature is around 45^0 Fahrenheit that would be about 7^0 Celsius. A good method for making sure you get the right temperature is to fill your ice bucket or any deep container is you don't have a special Remember that champagne that is too warm will foam and spill when you uncork the bottle. You'll lose some of the bubbles and make a mess.

1. Remove foil and Loosen Wire Cage – Take the foil off the top of the bottle the wire cage is totally free of foil. Leaving the wire cage in place will keep the cork in place until you're ready to remove it.
2. Use a Towel – With the bottle upright, drape a towel over the top of the bottle. With the towel there, even if the cork does pop out, it will be caught in the towel. It also catches any champagne that spills – if the uncorking ceremony is not perfect.

3. Turn the Champagne Bottle – Lay the then part of the towel draped bottle in your hand and get a good grip on the cork. Slowly turn the bottle while you hold onto the cork, don't yank the cork when you feel it loosen. Gently turn the bottle until you hear a little "pop". The noise comes from the carbon dioxide escaping. A loud pop means that you've let out too much carbon dioxide-usually along with a good bit of the champagne. The soft pop you'll hear means that you've preserved the bubbles in your champagne.
4. Pour the Champagne – The secret to pouring champagne is to pour just about an ounce or two fingers worth, of in into the glass. You'll want to use a tall champagne flute or tulip-shaped glass to get the best results. Wait for the initial foaming bubbles to subside, and then pour again until about two-thirds of the glass is full. This method will avoid the mess of the foam spilling over the sides of the glass. Keep the bottle in the ice bucket whenever you aren't pouring.

Meals as a part of Interviews

Employers may want to see you in a more social situation to see how you conduct yourself, particularly if the job which you are interviewing requires a certain standard of conduct with clients and superiors. You could be critically scrutinised on your table manners and conduct. On a practical level, interviews that last for several hours may extend through mealtimes, and the employer is acting as a gracious host to provide you with meals. The meal is a time to visit and interact, and this is always more important than the function of eating.

Party Lunches

A coffee or morning party may lead to a luncheon, which the hostess may arrange impromptu without much preparation. Certainly not all the guests may able to attend such an on the–spot lunch because they may have been already booked for other engagements. However, a friendly party may sometimes naturally lead to a lunch by the same host and hostess and those without other appointments may stay on. These guests should at once realise that a lunch is a more serious event are offering a major meal of the day and no matter how simple it may be, it must require more thorough and disciplined arrangements.

The switch from an ordinary party to a lunch party has to be attended by guests with some etiquettes that would make the lunch party, however in ostensible it may be a success. The first thing is personal cleanliness. Since the lunch is a bigger affair, the guests may retire and have a wash and make themselves more presentable after the sweat and heat and enjoyment of the earlier party. A hostess is always pleased to meet neat, clean and fresh looking people at her lunch-table. It would be the duty of the guests to take the lunch party not as an extension of the party they had but something new and fresh. They should, therefore, prepare themselves to take part in this new party (i.e. lunch).

This change-over from one party to another will naturally mean a different set of manners for the same guests and the talk and conversation or jokes, if at all, have to be on a subdued note. It is subdued in the sense that the note of the previous party cannot be continued in the lunch-room or while taking food and the guests has to bring out their lunch-time manners. Thus a new party is on the anvil and it may again be shaped according to the taste and inclinations of those participating in it. Sometimes when the guests and the host are equally adept in this art, they may bring themselves to talking on something quite different which may be suitable for a group of persons who are eating their food and little by little another party may be in full swing calling for different manners and actions.

Thus, it is like a change from one dance to another. The change from participation in one party to participation in another in the same premises or by the same host will have separate starts and finishes. In a morning party in which the guests had been participating, the guests and the hosts may come to behave very informally almost to the point of extracting enjoyment at the cost of one another since it is a friendly party and for their own enjoyment. At a lunch has to be cubed and in its place cooperation, politeness and mutual help will have to be generated. It is quite possible that while in the morning party one guest has deprived another of the last snack and the act had created amusement all-round, the same thing when done at a lunch party would appear to be the height of impoliteness and bad manners.

Some Tips on Eating Out

Importance of Table Manners

Table manners play an important part in making a favourable impression. They are visible signals of the state of our manner and therefore are essential to professional success. Regardless of whether we are having lunch with a prospective employer dinner with a business associate, our manners can speak volumes about us as professionals.

Napkin Use

The meal begins when the host unfolds his or her napkin. This is your signal to do the same. Place your napkin on your lap, completely unfolded if it is a small luncheon napkin or in half, lengthwise, if it is a large dinner napkin. Typically, you want to put your napkin on your lap soon after sitting down at the table (but follow your host's lead.) the napkin remains on your lap throughout the entire meal and should be used to gently blot your mouth when needed. If you need to leave the table during the meal, place your napkin on your chair as a signal to your server that you will be returning. The host will signal the end of the meal by placing his or her napkin on the table. Once the meal is over, you too should place your napkin neatly on the table to the right of your dinner plate. (Do not refold your napkin, but don't wad it up, either.)

Ordering

If, after looking over the menu, there are items you are uncertain about, ask your server any questions you may have Answering your questions is part of the server's job, it is better to find out before you order that a dish is prepared with something you do not like or are allergic to than to spend the entire meal picking tentatively at your food.

An employer will generally suggest that your order be taken first; his or her order will be taken last. Sometimes, however, the server will decide how the ordering will proceed. Often, women's orders are taken before men's.

As a guest, you should not order one of the most expensive items on the menu or more than two courses unless your host indicates that it is all right. If the host says, "I'm going to try this delicious sounding cheesecake; why don't you try dessert too," or "The prime rib is the speciality here; I think you'd enjoy it, "then it is all right to order that item if you would like.

"Reading" the Table Setting

Should you be attending a formal dinner or banquet with preset place settings it is possible to gain clues about what may be served by "reading" the place setting. Start by drawing an imaginary line through the centre of the serving plate (the plate will be placed in the centre of your dining space). To the right of this imaginary line all of the following will be placed; glassware, cup and saucer, knives, and spoons, as well as seafood fork if the meal includes seafood. It is important to place the glassware or cup back in the same position after its use in order to maintain the visual presence of the table. To the left of this imaginary line all of the following will be placed; bread and butter plate (including small butter knife placed horizontally across the pop of the plate), salad plate, napkin, and forks. Remembering the rule of "liquids on your right" and "solids on your left" will help in allowing you to quickly become familiar with the place setting.

Use of Silverware

Choosing the correct silverware from the variety in front of you is not as difficult as it may first appear. Starting with the knife, fork, or spoon that is farthest from your plate, work your way in, using one utensil for each course. The salad fork is on your outermost left, followed by your dinner fork. Your soup spoon is on your outermost right, followed by your beverage spoon, salad knife and dinner knife. Your dessert spoon and fork are above your plate or brought out with dessert. If you remember the rule to work from the outside in, you'll be fine.

There are two ways to use a knife and fork to cut and eat your food. They are the American style and the European or continental style. Either style is considered appropriate. In the American style, one cuts the food by holding the knife in the right hand and the fork in the lift hand with the fork tines piercing the food to secure it on the plate. Cut a few bite-size pieces of food, and then lay your knife across the top edge of your plate with the sharp edge of the blade facing in. Change your fork from your left your right hand to eat, fork tines facing up. (If you are left-handed, dip your fork in your left hand, tines facing up). The European or continental style is the same as the American style in that you cut your meal by holding your knife in your right hand while securing your food with your fork in your left hand, tines facing down, and the knife in your right hand. Simply eat the cut pieces of food by picking them up with your fork still in your left hand.

When you have Finished

Do not push your plate away from you when you have finished eating. Leave your plate where it is in the place setting. The common way to show that you have finished your meal is to lay your fork and knife diagonally across your plate. Place your knife and fork side by side, with the sharp side of the knife blade facing inward and the fork, tines down, to the left of the knife. The knife and fork should be placed as if they are pointing to the numbers 10 and 4 on a clock face. Make sure they are placed in such a way that they do not side off the plate as it is being removed. Once you have used a piece of silverware, never place it back on the table. Do not leave a spoon in a cup, either; place it on the saucer. You can leave a soup spoon in a soup plate Any unused silverware is simply left on the table.

Across Cultural Dining Etiquettes

In today's inter-reliant, international and culturally diverse world economy, cross—cultural differences can have an impact on business success. Both at an individual and organizational level understanding the value, etiquette and protocol of different cultures can positively influence your dealings in the worldwide marketplace.

A lack of cross—cultural awareness can result in misinterpretations which may cause offense. Such outcomes may end in your reputation being tarnished and your business objectives impacted. Cross—cultural understanding and appreciation of foreign etiquette is important for today's globe trotting business person to avoid such negative repercussions.

One area of importance in cross—cultural awareness is the different dining etiquettes of the world. Understanding dining etiquette can help international business people polish their conduct and behaviour while dining or entertaining.

Cross—cultural dining etiquette involves considering the following points:

1. Seating - is there a protocol as to who sits where? Should one wait to be seated? Is it acceptable etiquette for men/women to sit next to one another?
2. Eating - what utensils, if any, are used? Is it a knife and fork, hands or chopsticks? Is there any etiquette around using them?

3. Body language – how should one sit? Is it bad etiquette to rest elbows on the table? If seated on the floor what is the correct position?
4. Conversation – is the meal the proper place to engage in conversation? If so, is discussing business appropriated?
5. The Food – what foods are common to eat? Is it good etiquette to compliment the cook and how? Does one finish everything on the plate? Is it polite to ask for more.
6. Home/restaurant – what differences in etiquette or protocol would there be? Does one take a gift to the home? Who pays the bill at a restaurant?

By way of outlining some of the cross – cultural differences in dining etiquette across the world, the following countries shall be used as examples:

Dining Etiquette in Germany

1. It is good etiquette to remain standing until shown where to sit.
2. Table manners are continental-fork in left hand and knife in right.
3. Do not begin eating until the host signals to do so.
4. It is bad etiquette to rest elbows on the table.
5. Try and cut food with the fork as it complements the cook by showing it is tender.
6. Everything should be eaten on the plate.
7. Indicate you have finished by lying the fork and knife parallel across the right hand side of the plate.

Dining Etiquette in Japan

1. An honoured guest sits at the centre of the table furthest from the door and begins eating first.
2. Learn to use chopsticks-never point them, never pierce food with them, rest them on the chopstick rest when breaking for drink or chat.
3. It is good etiquette to try a bit of everything.
4. Conversation is subdued.

Dining Etiquette in Turkey

1. Meals are a social affair. Conversations are animate and loud.
2. The head of the family or honoured guest is served first.
3. It is good etiquette to insist the most senior is served first instead of you.
4. Asking for more food is a compliment.
5. If taken to a restaurant, Turkish dining etiquette has strict rule that the one who extended the invitation must pay.

Dining Etiquette in USA

1. The fork is held in the right hand and is used for eating.
2. To use the knife, the fork is switched to the left hand. To continue eating, the fork is switched back to the right hand.
3. If you are more comfortable eating in the continental manner it will not offend anyone.

4. Foods or drinks can be refused without causing offence.
5. Many foods are eaten by hand.

Dining Etiquette in Pakistan

1. Do not chew so loudly that someone else can hear it.
2. Chew with your mouth closed.
3. Eat everything on the plate; living some food is considered wasteful.
4. Eating additional servings is considered polite and a complement to the host.
5. When using a knife and fork, eat American style switching fork from left to right hand or keep knife in left hand.
6. Do not start eating until the eldest in the family eats first.
7. If eating good with bread, first bread in half. Then break off a small piece, only using your right hand if you can do so elegantly. Use bread to pinch or scoop food between thumb and fingers.

Dining Etiquette in India

1. Wait for the host or the eldest person to start first.
2. You should maintain silence while eating food. You are not expected to chat unnecessarily with the people around the table.
3. It is acceptable not to use cutlery for eating, as many food's - such as Indian breads and curry - are best enjoyed when eating with the hand.

4. Wash hands thoroughly before sitting at the table as some Indian foods are primarily eaten by hand. Also, wash hands after eating the food. Usually, a finger bowl (with luke warm water and lemon) is served per person for rinsing fingers.
5. In North India, when eating curry, the gravy must not be allowed to stain the fingers–only the fingertips are used. However, is South India, it is acceptable to use more of your hand.
6. When flatbreads such as chapatti, roti, or naan are served with the meal, it is acceptable and expected to use pieces of them to gather food and sop-up gravies and curries.
7. The cardinal rule of dining is to always use the right hand when eating or receiving food and never the left. Even a piece from the bread is broken using the right hand alone.
8. It is considered inappropriate to use your fingers to share food from someone else's plate once you have started using your own. Instead, ask for a clean spoon to transfer the food to your plate from the common dish.
9. When eating with hands, always eat with right, as mentioned above. However, use only the other clean hand to transfer food from a common dish on the table.
10. It is not necessary to taste each and every dish prepared; but you must finish everything on the plate as it is considered a respect for served food. For that reason, take only as much food on the plate you can finish.

Dining Etiquette in Malay

1. Footwear must not be worn in a Malay home due to hygienic reasons.
2. As a guest, if you feel that you cannot consume more food, it is courteous to turn it down by eating a small morsel or by graciously declining it altogether.
3. Remember that the right hand is always used for eating the traditional Malay way-Never the left hand since that it is considered unclean.
4. Have the oldest person served first (disregard whether it is male or female.)
5. Always cover your mouth when tooth picking.
6. Always turn your head away from the table if you are sneezing or coughing.
7. For functions that require guests to sit down on the floor, men should sit crossed-legged and not stretch them.
8. Pointing your feet at others is impolite-point your feet away from them.
9. You must leave some drinking beverage in the glass or cup after you finish drinking.
10. Never leave your plate dry after eating.
11. Don't hit or knock on an empty plate as it is considered calling the devils.
12. Do not put back dishes to its original place when you have taken it to your plate.
13. Do not talk when your mouth is full as it is considered rude.

Dining Etiquette in Middle East

1. Guests are honoured with prime choice to meets-head, eyes, etc.
2. Eaten with right hand only.
3. Meat is torn by holding down the piece against the dish and ripping off a desired amount with forefinger and thumb pressed together.
4. Rich is scooped up.
5. Do not be afraid of making a mess.
6. If you are finished leave food on your plate otherwise it will be filled immediately.
7. It is proper etiquette to compliment the host on the food and his hospitality.

The above are a very small number of examples of cross—cultural differences in dining etiquette. It is prudent to try and ascertain some facts about the dining etiquette of any country you plan to visit on business. By doing so you present yourself to the best of your ability and maximize the potential of your business trip.

❑❑❑

7
Business Etiquettes

Etiquette mean's conventional rules of polite behaviour'. Everywhere you work there will be other people inside and outside your organization who you deal with and it is crucial to talk with them well. A key part of this is to show you respect in the appropriate way, and conform to the largely unwritten guidelines on behaviours. The more you understand the rules, the more comfortable you will in any business circumstances.

Business etiquette is a coordination and communication function with emotional cohesion. With the development of society, the business relations are getting more and more extensive, and the variety of business contacts gradually has been forming general conducts and guidelines in the field of business as well as society.

Business etiquette is behavioural science, and should be seriously systemically trained. Due to geographical and historical backgrounds, it may have various kinds of differences, but it truly reflects the same aspiration, and to abide by the norms and codes of conduct as well.

Etiquette is very important to business. Understanding business etiquettes help you to deal confidently with your customers and business acquaintances. In today's increasingly culturally diverse workface, the chances of saying or doing "the wrong thing" become much greater than ever before. To change business environment demands that business people master the principles of etiquette in order to avoid the serious ramification of inappropriate behaviour, poor judgement, or cultural insensitivity.

Business etiquette cover up a very wide range of things:

1. How to behave as an individual?
2. How you make use of the communication tools available?
3. How you act in the team and company that you work in?
4. How you deal with external business contacts?

There are some general commandments of good manners that we all understand. Every company has slightly different conventions about appropriate conduct. Remember that when you start a job it's bit like joining a new club. Some of the rules might be written down but everyone else knows the other members and how to act with them. You have to learn it all if you are going to enjoy being there.

How professional are you?

In today's business structure, professionalism is measured by perceived social appropriateness for the work environment as it relates to a main component, the firm's image. The manner in which employees conduct themselves says a lot more than people tend to realize. In the same manner, employees need to be aware of how their behaviour in the workplace effects the business overall. Some examples related to professionalism include appearance, body language and attitude.

First impressions weigh heavily on determining confidence level. Customers use the first impression as a determinant of the trustworthiness of the business. Therefore, it is important to be aware of proper professionalism in business today. In order to measure the effects of professionalism, research is fundamental in determining the result of projecting professionalism, or the lack of professionalism, and how affects businesses today.

Appearance, body language, and attitude sure strong part of overall professionalism. According to read, appearance lends credibility and may help employers envision the staff member in a role with greater responsibility. Body language reflects confidence, capability and ability, string and effective body language can help establish and immediate rapport with your audience, signaling confidence in your message. Even though body language is considered a small percentage of communication; it is important to remember that communication is 55% visual and 38% vocal. Some of the best communicators today have strong body language in which they command attention and respect. Communicators that reflect professionalism are viewed from the outside as having charisma, being capable and confident.

Attitude is considered an interpersonal skill that many people in the workforce today should be aware of and understand how the effects whether positive or negative can affect the business. Attitude is cited as one of the most significant weaknesses in the workforce. It is now understood how critical this skill is with regard to how it affects once chances of advancement.

Human Resource managers are looking for employees who have interpersonal skills as part of their work ethic for jobs today. Appearance, body language and attitude are all prime components of professionalism. The ability to utilize all three components will help both the individual and firm.

Why do you need to know about business etiquette?

Business etiquette is very important today as many business relationships are over lunch or dinner. If you don't know how to act, it could be a deal breaker. How you look, act, speak and write gives people around you an impression. In business that first impression is significantly more important. The people you work with will see and speak to you frequently. Customers will expect helpfulness and civility when you meet them. Bosses will expect you to be courteous.

In the last 15 years workplaces have become much more informal most people are called by their first names, for instance and dress codes are much less rigid in many industries. There has been a removal of hierarchy and a move to flatter organizations with fewer supervisors and managers. This doesn't mean that less respectful behaviour towards others is sanctioned. It's just that the rules aren't so obvious.

What matters most is that your behaviour, dress, speech and other communication with your colleagues and customers other appropriate for your job and the company you work for. Business people often talk about 'networking', which is about building up ongoing relationships with contacts that may be useful in the future. Understanding. Good business etiquette is essential in setting up your own network and keeping it going.

Knowing how to behave, with politeness and courtesy, is a very important part of business life. Using business etiquette to create the right impression will determine not only how you enjoy each working day, but also your chances of promotion and success in your career.

Importance of Good Business Etiquettes

Etiquette is a very important factor in determining the success or failure of a business or a person; here are a few Tips on Business etiquettes. Etiquette is the way a person present himself to others, being comfortable and making other people around comfortable.

Good Business Etiquette – Recipe to Success

It is very important to practice good manners and etiquettes in order to succeed in your business, bit liked by people and maintain good relationships with clients, customers and employees.

When you do not practice good etiquettes intentionally or unintentionally, you are bound to face lot of obstacles on the path to success. But if a person is generally considerate and attentive to the needs of those who work for him/her by following the basic rules of etiquette, he/she will definitely be successful in any venture.

It is easier to make money than to earn respect and accolade from people who know and interact with you like colleagues and employees. Life will definitely be easier if you follow the following Tips on Business etiquettes.

1. Make sure to treat each person you interact with such as a secretary or a janitor, no matter what his or her position in the corporation, with respect and make it a rule to be pleasant to everybody no matter what the situation is.
2. Let people know that you appreciate what they do which will boost morale and improve work quality.
3. Keep records of people who matter to you and acknowledge if they receive a promotion and wish them on their birthdays.
4. When organising meetings make sure that all the participants know about the schedule, the objective of the meeting, matter that is to be discussed and the expected duration of the meeting.
5. Distribution of minutes and summaries of meetings and thanking each participant after meetings is a basic courtesy.
6. Always return calls, if you are unable to answer have a polite message on the answering machine that will be returned at the earliest. Never be rude or impatient with anyone on the phone.
7. Never make anyone wait, be it an employee or employer, or a business acquaintance. Never be late for a meeting or for work.
8. Dress is also a very important aspect in maintaining good business etiquette. Businessmen have to appear impeccably groomed.

9. Women have to dress appropriately and take care that do not give a wrong impression to their colleagues. Proper care taken can avert a lot of embarrassment.
10. Make sure your employees practice good etiquettes to customers and to each other to be able to work in a friction free atmosphere. Smiling courteous service will indicate your respect to others; understanding reception etiquettes, you will make your customers feel at ease; having a good professional mentality and appearance, good communication techniques and behaviour, with business etiquettes, the managers will gradually have a good professional qualities; understanding your–self and understanding others can strengthen the team spirits, which will finally greatly enhance the personal image as well as the company image. Here are some business etiquette tips which will help you to achieve the results in business activities and create better economic and social benefits for your company.

The Opportunity

Business etiquette is made up of significantly more important things than knowing which fork to use at lunch with a client. Unfortunately, in the perception of others, the devil is in the details. People may feel that is you can't be trusted not to embarrass yourself in business and social situations, you may lack the self-control necessary to be good at what you do. Etiquette is about presenting yourself with the kind of polish that shows you can be taken seriously. Etiquette is also about being comfortable around people (and making them comfortable around you!)

People are a key factor in your own and your business success. Many potentially worthwhile and profitable alliances have been lost because of an unintentional breach of manners.

The Solution

Most behaviour that is perceived as disrespectful, discourteous or abrasive is unintentional, and could have been avoided by practicing good manners or etiquette. We've always found that most negative experiences with someone were unintentional and easily repaired by keeping an open mind and maintaining open, honest communication. Basic knowledge and practice of etiquette is a valuable advantage, because in a lot of situations, a second chance may not be possible or practical.

There are many written and unwritten rules and guidelines for etiquette, and it certainly behooves a business person to learn them. The caveat is that there is no possible way to know all of them!

These guidelines have some difficulty to—navigate nuances, depending on the company, the local culture, and the requirements of the situation. Possibilities to commit a faux pas are limitless, and chances are, sooner or later, you'll make a mistake. But you can minimize them, recover quickly, and avoid causing a bad impression by being generally considerate and attentive to the concerns of others, and by adhering to the basic rules of etiquette. When in doubt, stick to the basics.

The Basics

The most important things to remember is to be courteous and thoughtful to the people around you, regardless of the situation. Consider other people's feeling, stick to your convictions as diplomatically as possible. Address conflict as situation-related than Apologies when you step on toes. You can't go too far wrong if you stick with the basics you learned in kindergarten. (Not that those basics are easy to remember when you're in a hard-nosed business meeting!)

This sound simplistic, but the qualities we admire most when we see them in people in leadership positions, those are the very traits we work so hard to engender in our children. If you always behave so that you would not mind your spouse, kids, or grandparents watching you, you're probably ding fine. Avoid raising your voice (surprisingly, it can be much more effective at getting attention when lower it!) using harsh or derogatory language toward anyone (present or absent), or interrupting. You may not get as much "airtime" in meetings at first, but what you do say will be much more effective because it carries the weight of credibility and respectability.

The following are guidelines and tips that we've found helpful for dealing with people in general, in work environments, and in social situations.

It's About People

Talk and visit with people. Don't differentiate by position or standing within the company. Secretaries and janitorial staff actually have tremendous power to help or hinder your career. Next time you need a document prepared or a conference room arranged for a presentation, watch how many people are involved with that process (you'll probably be surprised!) and make it a point to meet them and show your appreciation.

Make it a point to arrive ten or fifteen minutes early and visit with people that work near you. When you're visiting another site, linger over a cup of coffee and introduce yourself to people nearby. If you arrive early for a meeting, introduce yourself to the other participants. At social occasions, use the circumstances of the event itself know the host or how they like the crab dip. Talk a little about yourself—your hobbies, kids, or pets; just enough to get people to open up about theirs and get to know you as a person.

Keep notes on people. There are several "contact management" software applications that are designed for salespeople, but in business, nearly everyone is a salesperson in some capacity or another. They help you create a "people database" with names, addresses, phone numbers, birthdays, spouse and children's names whatever depth of information is appropriate for your situation.

It's good idea to remember what you can about people; and to be thoughtful. Send card or letters for birthdays or congratulations of promotions or other events, wend flowers for engagements, weddings or in condolence for the death of a loved one or family member. People will remember your kindness, probably much longer than you will!

Peers and Subordinates

Impressing the boss isn't enough.

Social rank class is a cornerstone of social interaction in may cultures. The corporate climate in the United States is no exception. People tend to feel uneasy until they've seen an "organisational chart" or figured out who reports to whom. They feel that it is more important to show respect and practice etiquette around superiors than around peers or subordinates.

The current social and economic climate is one of raped advancement through technology, which make it very possible (and even likely) for a pesky salesman to become an important client, or an administrative assistant to become a manager.

Mergers and acquisitions add to this "class mixing," causing a former competitor to become a coworker overnight. This can make things awkward if you treat people differently depending on their "corporate standing" if you show respect and courtesy to everyone, regardless of position or company, you avoid discomfort or damaging your chances in any unexpected turn of events.

Having a consistent demeanour improves your credibility. Even the people at the top will begin to suspect your motives if you treat VIPs with impeccable courtesy and snap at counter clerks.

Superiors

The only thing you owe your boss above and beyond what you won peers and subordinates if more information unobtrusively be sure he or she knows what you're doing, is alerted as early as possible to issues that may arise, and is aware of outcomes and milestones.

Never surprise your boss. It goes without saying that you should speak well of him or her within and outside the company, and give him or her benefit of the doubt.

International Business

Modern business is global and demands people travel to foreign countries and mix with foreign clients, colleagues or customers. Each one of those cultures will also have their own etiquette rules, many of them unwritten. When two or more different cultures mix, it is easy for small etiquette mistakes to be made that could have negative consequences. Jut as you may have felt annoyed when a foreign businessman did not shake your hands upon greeting you, imagine how your Chinese client must have felt when you wrote on his business card or your Indian colleague reacted when you flatly rejected an offer of a meal. Sometime, not understanding the etiquette of another culture means you show a lack of manners and a lack of deference. This can and does lead to soured relationships, lost deals and in the end poor business results. Anyone working on the international stage needs to understand international business etiquette.

It is important to note that etiquette in other cultures requires a bit of adaptation and flexibility. It you're travelling on business to a foreign destination, or have visitors here, it is a good idea to learn as much as you can about the culture they are coming from and make appropriate allowances.

International business etiquette manifests in many shapes and sizes. Throughout the would people from different cultures have varying etiquettes rule around areas such as personal space, communication gift giving, food, business meetings and much more. For those wanting to make a good impression and understanding of international business etiquette is crucial. By way of introducing some of the key areas within international business etiquette we shall look at the following common areas.

Business Card Etiquette

When you exchange business cards (even if you exchange them) do you simply pass it over and forget about it? in many countries the business card has certain etiquette rules. For example, in the Arab world you would never give or receive a business card with your left hand. In China and Japan you should try and use both hands to give and receive. In addition, it is always good etiquette to examine the card and make a positive comment on it. Whereas in the UK it may be OK to sling the business card into a pocket, in many countries you should always treat it with much more respect such as storing it in a business card holder.

The Etiquette of Personal Space

How close do you stand to people? Is it impolite to touch somebody? What about gender differences? In the middle–east you may get very touch-feely with the men, yet one should never touch a woman. A slap on the back may be OK in Mexico but in China is a serious no-no. Touch someone on the head in Thailand or Indonesia and you would have caused great insult. Without an appreciation of international business etiquette, these things would never be known.

The Etiquette of Gift Giving

Many countries such as China and Japan have many etiquette rules surrounding the exchange of business gifts. International business etiquette allows you an insight into what to buy, how to give a gift, how to receive, whether to open in front of the giver and what gifts not to buy, great examples of gifts to avoid are anything alcoholic in Muslim countries, anything with four of anything great in Japan and clocks in China.

The Etiquette of Communication

Some cultures like to talk loudly (US and Germany), some softly (India and China); some speak directly (Holland

and Denmark) others indirectly (UK and Japan); some tolerate interrupting other while speaking (Brazil) others not (Canada); some are very blunt (Greece) and some very flower (Middle East). All will believe the way they international context this no longer applies. Without the right international business etiquette it is easy to offend.

Items to consider:

- Language (make an effort to learn theirs if possible, but don't pretend to be fluent unless you have many years of study under your belt!)
- Time zones
- Working schedules
- Holidays
- Food customs (table manners, use of implements, etc.)

By way of conclusion we can state that etiquette helps maintain good relation with people. When dealing with people from a shared culture, everyone knows the rules and there is not much to think about. Those that lack etiquette are branded as uncouth and rude. However, this is not the same when working on the international stage. Someone may very well come across as being rude through a lack of etiquette but this may be because in their culture that behaviours is normal. As a result international business etiquette is a key skill for those wanting to be successful when working abroad. Through a great appreciation and understanding of other's cultures you build stronger and linger lasing business relationships.

Meetings

If a subject is important enough to call a meeting, be considerate of the participants time and ensure that it is well prepared.

Business meetings are one arena in which poor etiquette can have negative effects. By improving your business meeting etiquette you automatically improve your chances of success. Comfort, trust, attentiveness and clear communications are examples of the positive results of demonstrating good etiquette.

The piece of writing will focus on a few key examples of business meeting etiquette for both formal and informal business meeting etiquette for both formal and informal business meetings.

Informal Meeting

Informal meetings are generally more relaxed affairs and may not necessarily take place in the office or meeting room. Even so a sense of professionalism and good business etiquette are still required. There are some points to consider with informal meetings:

1. Business etiquette demands that the person calling the meeting (henceforth 'the chair') should be the most senior or the one with the most direct or urgent interest in the topic at hand.
2. The chair should decide the time, place and agenda. These details should be confirmed with everyone to make sure all the are in agreement and no inconvenience is caused.
3. The chair must make the purpose of the meeting clear to the attendees, how ling it will last and what

is expected of them, i.e. particular information or preparation of documents. Failing to relay the proper information is bad business etiquette as it could cause embarrassment.

4. Punctuality is a must. Keeping people waiting is considered the height of poor etiquette as it abuses their time.
5. The chair should strive to ensure the meeting stays within a set framework or agenda so that it is kept as short and effective as possible. He/she must keep circular disagreements and the like to a minimum.
6. The chair should (pre-) appoint someone to record the proceedings; documenting major decisions or action points. This can later be distributed to the attendees for reference.
7. If the results of the meeting have no effect on others who were not present it is considered proper business etiquette to inform them.

Formal meetings

The business etiquette of formal meetings such as departmental meetings, management meetings, board meetings, negotiations and the like can be puzzling. Such meetings usually have a set format. For example, the chair may always be the same person, minutes, agendas or reports may be pre-distributed or voting may take place. Here are some business etiquette guidelines that are applicable to any formal meeting:

1. Prepare well for the meeting as your contribution may be integral to the proceedings. If you are using

statistics, reports or any other information make sure if has been handed out at least three days prior to the meeting.

2. Dress well and arrive in good time. Your profession is linked to both.
3. Always remember to switch of a mobile phone.
4. If there is an established seating pattern, accept it. If you are unsure, ask.
5. Acknowledge any introductions or opening remarks with a brief recognition of the chair and other participants.
6. When discussions are under way it is good business etiquette to allow more senior figures to contribute first.
7. Never interrupt anyone-even if you disagree strongly. Note what has been side and return to it later with the chair's permission.
8. When speaking, be brief and ensure what you say is relevant.
9. Always address the chair unless it is clear that others are not doing so.
10. It is a serious breach of business etiquette to divulge information to other about a meeting. What has been discussed should be considered as confidential.

The underlying principles of all the above business meeting etiquette pointers are good manners, courtesy and consideration. If these principal are adhered to the chances of offense and misunderstandings are greatly reduced.

Email

Since so much business is now conducted via email, understanding business email etiquette is of great value, a few guidelines to keep in mind are to know one's audience, keep communication short and to the point, and keep business email similar to business email similar to regular business email, within these guidelines for business email etiquette there several exceptions.

If one is responding to a job query or a business post, be certain to ascertain when possible whether to an ad for a job should be essentially a cover litter. Most ads will state whether or attach a resume or cut and paste the resume.

Some companies will not open attachments and will delete email with attachments.

As well, when an attachment is acceptable, be certain it is not of great length. Sending anything over 150k is most cases. However, a project that two people are working on together may occasionally require graphics or project files that take up more space. Simply ascertain whether the business associate whishes these to be sent via email. He or she may prefer a snail disc copy to cut down on how long it take an email to load.

Business email etiquette suggests using formality in addressing people. In general, address people as one addresses someone as Mr. Sharma, don't begin a letter by using Mr. Sharma's first name. If one usually calls Mr. Sharma by his first name, business email etiquette allows for the formal address.

Where one is unfamiliar with the married status of a female, business email to doctors. In this case use the formal title of Dr.

Be certain to include a specific subject line regarding the contents of one's email. This could be "Reply to job posting #1351 on Craig's List," Let's meet this week to discuss our options." Make certain the subject reflects the material one intends to present.

Business email does not need creative punctuation, smiley faces or other flourishes that might occur in casual email between friends. It should also be free of chat abbreviations. Two close business associates might include them in their emails, but generally formal is better.

To cut down to space, do not quote all material sent by someone else. Cut, paste, and quote only short bits of material when relevant. If the material before replying to a message. As well, keep one's won material short and to the point.

Business email etiquette further requires one to communicate using good grammar, well-constructed sentences and properly spelled words. If one is not strong in these areas, communications can look fairly foolish and make one seem less intelligent. Be certain to spell and grammar check material, and then read it over again, out a problem, loud, to verify it makes sense. If grammar still remains a problem, consider a course in business writing to help improver written communication.

Lastly, do not add business associates to one's joke list. This is a clear violation of business email etiquette. If one works with some who enjoys jokes, ask for their private email to add to one's list. As well, never forward chain mail to a business associate. If one receives a virus warning, check internet hoax sites prior to sending this on to business associates. Most virus warnings sent by email the hoaxes and cause unnecessary alarm, or take up space in what should be a business-oriented mailbox.

Phone

Always return calls. Even if you don't have an answer to the caller's question, call and explain what you're doing to get the requested information, or direct them to the appropriate place to get it.

If you're going to be out, have someone pick up your calls or at a minimum, have your answering system tell the caller when you'll be back in the office and when they can expect a call back.

When you initiate a call and get a receptionist or secretary, identify yourself and tell them the basic nature of your call. That way, you'll be sure you're getting the right person or department and the person you're trying to reach will be able to pull up the appropriate information and help you more efficiently.

When you're on the receiving end to a phone call, identify yourself and your department. Answer the phone with some enthusiasm or at least warmth, even if you are being interrupted, the person on the other end doesn't know that!

Make sure your voice mail system is working properly and doesn't tell the caller that the mailbox is full, transfer them to nowhere, or ring indefinitely. Address technical and system problems – a rude machine or system is as unacceptable as a rude person.

You don't have to reply to obvious solicitations. If someone is calling to sell you something, you can indicate that you are not interested and hang up without losing too much time on it. However, you do need to be careful. You may be receiving a call from an insurance or long distance company that wants to hire you as a consultant! Be sure you know the nature of the call before you (politely, of course) excuse yourself.

Personalise the conversation. Many people act in electronic media (including phone, phone mail, and e-mail) the way they cast in their care. They feel since they're not face-to-face with a person, it is perfectly acceptable to be abrupt, crass, or rude. We need to ensure that we make best use of the advantages of these media without falling headfirst into the disadvantages.

Interruptions

Avoid interruptions (of singular or group work sessions, meetings, phone calls, or even discussions) if at all possible. Most management folks feel free to interrupt informal working sessions of subordinates, but need to realise that they may be interrupting a brainstorming session that will produce the company's next big success.

Always apologies if must interrupt a conversation, meeting, or someone's concentration on a task. Quickly state the nature of what you need, and show consideration for the fact that you are interrupting valuable work or progress.

Guests, Consultants and New Employees

If you have a new employee, guest, or consultant working at you company for a day, week, or longer, be sure that person has the resources and information that he or she needs to do the job. This isn't just courtesy, it's good business, since time spent flailing around looking for things is embarrassing to the consultant and expensive for your company.

Give a consultant or guest the same type of workspace as an employee at your company in a similar role. A consultant who is there to do programming should have, if at all possible, the same size cube, type of computer equipment, etc. as an employee programmer would have in your company. This prevents your employees from feeling looked down-upon, and the consultant from feeling singlled out or treated as second-rate.

A guest from a regulatory agency will tend to want to know what's "really" going on in the company. By treating him or her lime everyone else, (instead of isolation them in a plush office in a far wing, for example) will raise less suspicion and enable them to get the information they need more efficiently.

Appoint as employee to be a "buddy" to a guest or consultant to ensure that they are introduce around, "shown the ropes," and have someone to help resolve little logistical problems that may arise and cause non-productivity or embarrassment.

Appreciation

Always pass along credit and compliments to everyone who made a contribution to the effort. Speak well or your coworkers and always point out their accomplishments to any interested party. Appearing to have taken the credit in a superiors' or customers' eye is the surest way to sabotage a relationship with a coworker.

Dress/Appearance

It can be insulting to your coworkers or clients to show a lack of concern about your appearance. Being wrinkled, unshaven, smelly or unkempt communicates (intentionally or not) that you don't care enough about the situation, the people or the company to present yourself respectably. Here are some dress etiquettes for men and women:

Interview Attire for Women

1. **Were a Suit –**

   Although women have come a long way in the world of work, skirt suits are still preferred. There is an old saying "Dress the position you want, not the one you have." Many corporate offices follow the professional look their customers are accustomed to working with and placing confidence in. Longstanding colours such as Blue, Black, Gray, or Brown are the colour choice of many executive champions.

   The trick is to look conservative and professional Wear an appropriate length skirt, avoid tight skirts and mini-skirts. Let quality of your suit, followed by the strength of your works to impress your potential employer:

2. **Blouses –**

   A cotton or silk blouse in a neutral colour with a simple collar is fine. Do not wear a sleeve-less blouse, just in case you have to take off your jacket. Most conservative offices do not allow sleeveless blouses as proper dress attire. Be sure, to ask about the corporate culture of an office prior rushing out to the interview. With the rise and fall of dot.com companies, much has changed. Make sure your power wardrobe is for the correct setting. Your blouse should fit comfortably, and not appear to be tight, wrinkled or distracting due to loud colours.

3. **Scarves –**

   A classic 34-inch square silk scarf that compliments your suit in colour and less patterns. Keep it simple

4. **Shoes –**

   Pumps with 11/2 inch heel are standard. Choose a colour that compliments your suit and handbag black, brown, burgundy or navy. Avoid open-toe shoes, his boots, stiletto heels and white shoes. Be sure to have your shoes polished and shined and that your heels are in tact. Were leather shoes, avoid suede and light fabrics-they attract dust.

5. **Stockings –**

   If you wear a light coloured suit, wear light coloured stockings. Do not wear contrasting colours. Avoid opaque and printed stockings.

6. **Jewelry and Perfume –**

   Large hoop, dangling earrings should be left at home. Were small stubs or avoid wearing earrings. Do not wear more than one pair of earrings and two finger rings, one watch or bracelet. Remove all non traditional jewelry e.g. nose rings, eyebrow rings, multiple earrings.

Basic Rules:

1. When meeting with clients or other business associates, whether in your office or theirs, you should dress appropriately – if they wear suits – you wear one. When in doubt of your client's dress policy, traditional business attire is appropriate.
2. All business attire, whether traditional or casual should be reflective of a professional, dignified appearance. To reinforce our traditional business dress attire, men should wear business suits/blazers/sports coats, dress shirts and ties. Women should wear business suits/blazers, either skirted or pants; or dresses.

Interview attire for men

1. **Wear a Suit –**

   Unless you're interviewing in a field where a suit would look out of place, wear one. At most places, an open-collar shirt and suit jacket is fine. Were dark colour: blue, black, brown, gray.

2. **Shirts –**

   As a rule, the simpler the better, no bright colours, French cuffs or monograms. White, off white, pale, blue shirts are preferred: you can't go wrong with a cotton shirt.

3. **Ties –**

   To play it safe choose a traditional silk tie, no loud colours or patterns. Your tie should coordinate with your attire. It may also be wise to avoid ties with images and designer logos.

4. **Socks -**

   Choose a colour that coordinates with your suit (usually black, dark gray, dark brown, or dark blue) and make sure they are ling enough not to expose your skin when you sit down.

5. **Shoes -**

   Make sure your shoes are polished and shined and that your heels are in tack. Avoid wearing boots, wear dress shoes that coordinates with your attire.

7. **Jewelry and Cologne -**

   Less is better. Avoid wearing a lot of cologne and jewelry. Do not wear more than one ring, remove earrings and multiple chains.

Casual Business Attire Guidelines

1. Aim for a classic and understated look when selecting your casual business wear for the day. Pick clothing that is comfortable yet communicates a professional attitude. Subtle, quality accessories (belts, jewelry and scarves) coordinated with an outfit can show that you pay attention to impotent details.
2. Combine some of your existing business wardrobe with casual attire; for example, try wearing a button down shirt with khakis and loafers. Ask yourself, "Am I successfully representing myself and employer?"
3. Clothing should be clean, pressed or wrinkle free, and without holes or frayed areas. Shirts need to be tucked in (certain women's blouses are make to be worn out, however, and this is permitted.

4. Body piercing which can be seen by the client (with the exception of earrings) is not permitted. Tongue rings should not be visible.
5. Hairstyle should project a professional appearance: clean, neatly trimmed and well-groomed.
6. Pay attention the fit your clothing. Slams should break just above the shoe, sleeves should reach the base of your hand and just show a bit of the cuff if you are wearing a jacket, and shirt collars should button comfortably without pinching or leaving gaps.
7. If you wear a tie, its tip should reach below the bottom of your belt-buckle.
8. Shoes matter. Shoes should be polished and leather is generally preferred.
9. Take your day's schedule into account when you are dressing. Do not make assumptions. Keep a spare jacket, in the office for unexpected meetings.
10. When in doubt, leave it out. Casual clothing should make you and everyone you work with more comfortable while, at the same time, projecting a professional image.

Social Settings

Many impressions formed during a party, dinner or golf game can make or break a key business arrangement, whether or not business is discussed directly. Always carry business cards. Arrive at a party at the stated time or up to 30 minutes lager. (Not earlier than the stated time, under any circumstances.)

Business Etiquettes in India

Etiquettes refer to norms and standards for behaviour that is socially acceptable and being comfortable around people. Research conducted shows that technical skills and knowledge accounts for only 15% of getting, keeping and advancing in a job. 85% of the job success is connected to people skills.

This research significantly conclude the importance of etiquette skills that includes courtesy, image, trust and reliability; which increases opportunities for new business, fosters congenial business relationship, builds confidence and creates goodwill. India is one of the largest and most multi—cultured country and business culture here tends to be more informal and friendly.

Certain personality traits of Indian are:

1. There are more than 14 major and 300 minor languages spoken in India. The official languages are English and Hindi. English is widely used in business and education. Many Indians are vegetarians.
2. Indian often over promise in an effort to please.
3. Favourite topics of conversation are Politics, Family, Cricket, Bollywood and Films. Whistling is considered as Impolite.
4. Alcohol is usually avoided at lunch; Indian women are not always comfortable drinking in public.
5. Breakfast and dinner meetings are rare and usually business lunch is preferred.
6. Business decisions are mostly made at higher level.
7. The country's most important festival is Diwali, when business associate exchange small gifts, sweets or dry

fruits. It is considered especially auspicious to start a new business at this time.

However, general business etiquettes in India are:

1. Gifts are not opened in the presence of the giver.
2. Acceptable gifts are flowers, chocolates and perfumes.
3. "I will try" is an acceptable refusal rather than "No".
4. Putting hands on hips is rude.
5. Keeping confidential matters/materials in few hands as it can be used against the interest of the company. "In modern world if the company is able to deal e-mails effectively then they can gain competitive edge and achieve professionalism. While replying to e-mail include the original mail in your reply, in other words click "reply" instead of "new mail".

Make your subject line specific, meaningful and don't type in all CAPS as it signifies a scream", advices Mr. Hemant Parekh, CEO – Parekh Constructions Ltd, "Avoid glaring errors such as misspelling, proper grammar and punctuations as it can sometimes change the meaning of the text. Customise your mail and be concise, to the point" he added. Don't attach unnecessary files/document's in your e-mail; take care with abbreviations and emotions.

Use proper structure and layout; use active instead to passive voice, avoid long sentences and repetitive use of words like urgent and important. Never write e-mail to discuss confidential information; answer swiftly; don't reply to spam and never copy attachments or messages without permission are some e-mail etiquettes.

For effective meetings, communicate beforehand the objective, expected duration and the topics/issues expected to be discussed. Make it a point to arrive 10-15 minutes early for a meeting and introduce yourself to the other participants. A shout and light, not firm handshake is the customary start of the meeting and a non-verbal clue of friendly deal. Make sure to thank the meeting members for their time and participation; show them how their contribution helped to achieve the objective of the meeting. Avoid arranging your cell phones to meetings. There are certain telephone etiquettes which one need's to follow. Communication over phone requires the use of non-verbal skills such as pleasant tone, sweet voice, proper intonation and clear articulation of words. Before initiating a call, prepare yourself about what is your purpose and contents.

A confident self-introduction always makes a positive impression. Introduce yourself in a slow, clear manner and don't use words such as Mr., Ms., Mrs., Shri, Smt while referring to yourself, you can call other persons by such name. The most important things to remember is to be considerate, courteous, diplomatic and thoughtful to the people around you regardless of the circumstances. Address conflicts as situation related rather than people related and never differentiate the people by position or standing with the company. Treat all colleagues with respect and recognition.

Always speak well, don't leak other's secret and pass along credit to everyone who make a contribution to the efforts. REMEMBER-Don't take credit for your co-workers contribution to a project". Avoid chewing gums loudly and asking personal questions colleagues about their family size, marital status and religion; never tell dirty jokes or forward dirty e – mails.

Don't talk about your organization, other colleagues or boss behind their backs – as it minimizes irritation and contributes a positive work environment. For any business party carry your business card, avoid drinking too much and never use foul language or tell dirty jokes.

Don't wear suggestive, revealing clothes, and never do back-biting. "Always consider the languages, time zone, working schedule, holidays, food, tradition and customs of other country for any International Business as these have become critical elements of all global business managers. Thus, the basic knowledge and practices of etiquette is a valuable advantage because in lot of situations a second chance may not be possible. Finally, even work place has certain unwritten/written rules which apply to every single aspect of work life i.e. how to e-mail, talk on phone; conduct themselves in a meeting, business party and group conversation.

Business etiquette is essentially about building relationships with colleagues, clients or customers. In the business would, it is these people that can influence your success of failure. More and more companies, organisations put much attention on etiquette training. Practicing all the following tips on business etiquettes will have a remarkable effect in improving business and build contacts necessary for you business.

❑❑❑